THE *Analects* consists of sayings attributed to Master Kong (Confucius) and some of his disciples, some of which are set in the context of brief anecdotes. Master Kong's traditional dates are 551–479 BC and, although the authenticity of none of the sayings can be considered certain and some of the material it contains is clearly late, alien, or even hostile, the *Analects* is regarded as the repository of the earliest teachings of the Master. In view of the profound influence which Master Kong and the books associated with his name and with his school have had on Chinese ethical and political thought and on the nature of the Chinese state, this is an extremely important book.

RAYMOND DAWSON is an Emeritus Fellow of Wadham College, Oxford. He was Editor of *The Legacy of China* (1964) and his other publications include *The Chinese Chameleon: An Analysis of European Conceptions of Chinese Civilization* (1967); *Imperial China* (1972); *The Chinese Experience* (1978); *Confucius* (Past Masters, 1982); and *A New Introduction to Classical Chinese* (1984).

THE WORLD'S CLASSICS

CONFUCIUS

The Analects

Translated with an Introduction and Notes by
RAYMOND DAWSON

Oxford   New York
OXFORD UNIVERSITY PRESS

Oxford University Press, Walton Street, Oxford OX2 6DP

Oxford New York
Athens Auckland Bangkok Bombay
Calcutta Cape Town Dar es Salaam Delhi
Florence Hong Kong Istanbul Karachi
Kuala Lumpur Madras Madrid Melbourne
Mexico City Nairobi Paris Singapore
Taipei Tokyo Toronto

and associated companies in
Berlin Ibadan

Oxford is a trade mark of Oxford University Press

Translation, Editorial material © Raymond Dawson 1993

First published as a World's Classics paperback 1993

British Library Cataloguing in Publication Data
Data available

Library of Congress Cataloging in Publication Data
Confucius.
[Lun yü. English]
The analects / translated with an introduction and notes by
Raymond Dawson.
p. cm.—(World's classics)
Includes bibliographical references.
I. Dawson, Raymond. II. Title. III. Series.
PL2478.L34 1993 181'.112—dc20 92–46274
ISBN 0-19-283091-0

5 7 9 10 8 6 4

Printed in Great Britain by
BPC Paperbacks Ltd
Aylesbury, Bucks

CONTENTS

CONTENTS

INTRODUCTION

THE *Analects* consists of about 500 short pieces, generally known in English as chapters although they are rarely more than a few lines long. They are organized into twenty books. The contents are sometimes loosely described as the sayings of Confucius, who is generally referred to in the book as Master Kong. This is the term I shall use in this translation instead of Confucius, which is a Latinization of Kong fuzi (meaning 'this Master Kong' or 'the Master Kong'), which was first used in the Latin versions of the Jesuit translators 400 years ago, and has remained fashionable although we now write in the vernacular. In fact, although the contents consist largely of sayings of Master Kong, some occurring in isolation and some set in the context of brief anecdotes, the work also includes some chapters in which Master Kong plays no part. These chapters mainly consist of sayings and anecdotes concerning some of Master Kong's disciples. A few of these are themselves referred to as Master, which has suggested that the work was originally compiled by disciples of the Master's own disciples. For reasons of style and content it is fairly obvious that the *Analects* includes material composed at different periods: some chapters, for example, paint a picture of Master Kong which is that of the hagiographer, and some chapters are written in an artificial and literary style which is alien to the brief interchanges which were characteristic of what seems to be the oldest stratum. It is not easy to make clear-cut judgments about such issues, but more information is given in the Explanatory Notes as well as in the Note on the Text.

The traditional dates for the birth and death of Master Kong are 551 and 479 BC. Unfortunately our knowledge of Chinese history before 221 BC, when the Qin Dynasty brought about the unification of China, is not very precise and detailed, so that, for example, the editors of the multi-volume *Cambridge History of China* decided that their first volume would begin with the Qin. They were partly deterred

by the fact that a wealth of information, derived from the
enormous amount of archaeological activity which has taken
place in China in recent decades, remains to be co-ordinated;
but on the other hand nothing can compensate for the
shortage of texts from the pre-Qin period. Although collec-
tions of poetry and documents (known in English as the
Book of Songs and the *Book of Documents*) together with
some annalistic accounts and descriptions of ritual existed
in Master Kong's time, the *Analects* was first put together
before the techniques of continuous prose composition had
developed. The organization of the material is rudimentary,
and there are even places where fragments from alien sources
have been inserted into the text.

For those readers who are totally unfamiliar with ancient
Chinese history it is necessary to make a very brief introduction to the historical background. Although Master Kong
and his contemporaries believed in the existence of certain
ancient sage-kings who lived in remote antiquity, they were
particularly conscious of the more recent framework provided
by the so-called Three Dynasties, which are mentioned in the
Analects. These are the Xia (which from our point of view is
still legendary), the Yin, also known as the Shang (which is
famous for its superb sacrificial bronzes and for the writings
in a more pictographic version of the Chinese language
which appeared on oracle bones), and finally the Zhou. The
latter commenced at some time in the eleventh century BC,
when the Yin, whose capital was at Anyang, were overthrown by a less cultured people from the west. The Zhou
soon acquired the trappings of culture and the ruler who laid
the foundations of the dynasty was posthumously known as
King Wen (the cultured king). He was succeeded by King
Wu (the martial king), who was the actual founder of the
dynasty, and he by his son King Cheng, but since the latter
was still a boy the reins of power were in the hands of his
uncle, the Duke of Zhou, a younger brother of King Wu.

The early Zhou period was apparently looked upon by
Master Kong as a golden age, the Zhou having obtained the
Mandate of Heaven to replace the bad last ruler of the
Yin. It was believed that much of North China had been

controlled by the Zhou rulers and their allies. But Master
Kong and his contemporaries were conscious that a long
decline had set in. Although the Zhou Dynasty was nominally
still in existence, already by the seventh century BC the state
of Qi under Duke Huan was heading an alliance of virtually
independent northern Chinese states, whose ostensible role
was to support the now enfeebled house of Zhou, although
in reality their main concern was to offer united opposition
to the growing menace of the state of Chu which, originating
in the Yangtze valley, had rapidly spread in a northerly
direction. Master Kong's own state, Lu, was part of this
northern alliance, but in his own time even the rulers of Lu
were in their turn ousted by the powerful Three Families,
who are mentioned a number of times in the *Analects*. In the
circumstances Master Kong is depicted as looking back with
longing to the golden age of the early Zhou period when the
Way prevailed.

In the last sentence, as frequently elsewhere in this book, I
wrote 'depicted as', since it is necessary to be constantly
aware that one cannot claim with absolute certainty that any
of the 'sayings' come out of the mouth of Master Kong. At
the same time, of course, it cannot be clear to what extent he
imposed his own ideas on the early Zhou period. It has been
a long-standing practice in China to play safe by putting
praise and blame of people and institutions into a historical
disguise, and since there was no awareness of other great
civilizations, there was no alternative to setting Utopian
visions in remote antiquity. I do not think that it would be
profitable to go into the question of Master Kong's own life,
except in so far as it is necessary for an understanding of the
Analects. What used to be the standard history of Chinese
philosophy went so far as to declare that 'more is known
about the life of Confucius than of any other early Chinese
philosopher', but since this is due to the existence of a biography by Sima Qian, who not only enjoyed a good story
but also lived nearly five centuries later, we can safely dis-
miss this claim. Unfortunately long before this time fancy
had replaced fact, and Sima Qian's biography contains an
abundance of fantastic stories. His ancestry was predictably

princely, inevitably he had a meeting with Lao Zi, the shadowy figure who was the reputed founder of Daoism and, like all sages, he had a remarkable birth and extraordinary physical features. Nor do I, being incorrigibly sceptical and even disinclined to believe everything I read in the obituaries in this morning's newspapers, feel disposed to go along with those who take the view that anything written within 200 years of the Master's death should be taken seriously.

It is not surprising that Master Kong should have appeared in a variety of guises both in China and the West. In China this unbookish person became the patron of scholarship and this agnostic became a god. The Western versions have ranged from the patron saint of the Enlightenment to the comic character uttering his platitudes in pidgin English and unable to pronounce the letter 'r'. From the evidence of the *Analects* itself he was for the most part a teacher who tried to prepare men for public office. As a young man he seems to have held various minor posts, but although he would have liked to have held high office himself if it gave him the opportunity to introduce his own teachings, reports that he held senior positions and even became chief minister of Lu were later inventions. He spent time during the years 497 to 484 travelling in other states, but he returned to spend the evening of his life in Lu. Socially he was probably a member of the *shi* (public servant) class, which was the lowest of the three categories of people who filled posts in the government (see Note on the Translation of Key Terms, no. 6). But because of the appeal of his teaching and personality he acquired a reputation out of all proportion to his worldly success, so that after his death there were those who treasured his sayings.

The real breakthrough for Master Kong and the *Analects* came in the Han Dynasty. During the harsh and short-lived Qin Dynasty (221–206 BC) much ancient literature had been destroyed as a result of the notorious episode of the burning of the books in 213, especially when this measure (whose purpose was to deprive the community of all writings other than the Qin annals and works of purely practical value and to monopolize learning for the benefit of the state) was followed by a conflagration which wrecked the palace library, thus consuming the volumes kept solely for court scholars. As the Han Dynasty developed an enormous empire, a huge civil service was needed to run it and in 124 BC, during the time of the Emperor Wu (who reigned from 141 to 87 BC), an imperial academy was founded in which students were trained and given final examinations. These were the remote forerunners of the civil service examination system which was to dominate recruitment for the last thousand years of the Chinese empire. So although the Han was not a period when one single school of thought was able to obliterate the rest, it is clear that in the latter part of the Former Han Dynasty, which came to an end in AD 9, Confucianism held the premier position. Indeed the bibliographical chapter of the *History of the Former Han Dynasty* gives especial prominence to Confucianism, placing the *Analects* already in the first section, which is devoted to the hallowed category of the Classics, and putting the Confucians at the head of the second section which also included the various other philosophical schools. This was certainly a time when the gradual Confucianization of the Chinese bureaucracy was beginning to take place.

After the collapse of the Han Dynasty early in the third century AD China suffered a period of division during which Confucianism was eclipsed at the political level, but continued to play an important role in local communities. Buddhism gradually became the dominant philosophy, and although the restoration of unity by the Sui Dynasty in 589 AD revived the need for Confucian political thought and state examinations were even reintroduced in 606 AD, nevertheless Buddhism remained powerful throughout the Sui and Tang Dynasties. It was not until the Song Dynasty, which started in AD 960 that an extremely sophisticated civil service recruitment system based on Confucian texts became the established pattern. This persisted until 1905, except for a break under the Yuan (Mongol) Dynasty. The Song Dynasty was also famous as the period of the most distinguished Neo-Confucian philosophers. When things went wrong in China, there was always a tendency to believe that this was because the

authentic message of Master Kong was not properly understood. Hence the fresh look at Confucian philosophy which
was already prominent in the Tang period and grew to
maturity during the Song, partly stimulated by Buddhist
ideas. Even during the twentieth century there was an attempt
by the infant Republic of China to resist the pressure of
Western values by adopting Confucianism as a state religion.
More recently still the growing interest in Confucian thought
has in some cases been partly stimulated by the belief that
this creed might have the solution to problems which Western
values have conspicuously failed to solve.

But not only did the text of the *Analects* and other works
which had become associated with the name of Master Kong
secure survival and prestige. At the same time Master Kong's
own lasting glory was ensured by the fact that it became the
practice in ancient China for trades to have patron deities,
so he was the obvious person for the literati to worship,
which they did from the Tang Dynasty onwards in Confucian
temples throughout the country. The descendants of Master
Kong were also honoured and enjoyed vast estates, hundreds
of servants, and their own private army. Such luxury persisted
even into the present century, but Master Kong's descendants
have now had to accept the destiny of ordinary mortals.
Indeed not very long ago the current head of the family, a
seventy-seventh generation descendant of the Master, lectured
in Oxford and distributed mementoes of the occasion in the
form of ties which depicted the sage riding in a carriage
together with a quotation from the *Book of Changes* in
archaic Chinese script.

As the most authentic account of the teachings of this man
who was at the summit of Chinese intellectual life for 2,000
years the *Analects* is a work of great importance. But in
view of the nature of its compilation and the fact that it is
a human weakness to change one's mind, the attempt to
draw from it a consistent and well-rounded philosophy is a
risky enterprise, although it has understandably often been
attempted. To succeed it is necessary either to discard or to
stretch the meaning of passages which do not fall in with the
main thrust of the teachings. Moreover, to show any devel-

opment in the thought of Master Kong from his youth to his old age is of course very difficult as is also any attempt to unravel the sequence of composition of the various books. I will therefore content myself with some very general observations and leave those who wish to consider the philosophy further to attempt some of the works mentioned in the Select Bibliography.

The general observations which any reader of the *Analects* must bear in mind are the following. (1) Many of the brief utterances found in *The Analects* may be seen as seminal expressions of some of the typical ideas of Chinese civilization. This is the main importance of the work, as I have tried to show in some of my explanatory notes. (A more detailed exploration of this theme may be found in my book *Confucius*, which was written for the Past Masters series.) (2) The most novel feature of the morality of the *Analects* is that it contains the earliest use of humaneness (*ren*) as a philosophical term. Another innovation is the use of the 'Way' to summarize Master Kong's political ideal. The importance of these words is described in more detail in the Note on the Translation of Key Terms (see nos. 9 and 18). (3) The earliest parts of the *Analects* are the earliest writings emanating from Chinese civilization which deal primarily with ethical matters for their own sake and feature man's inclination to act for ethical reasons rather than for reasons of practical advantage. This is an important breakthrough in the history of Chinese thought. (4) Master Kong is not depicted as striving to analyse ethical terms in the manner of much Western moral philosophy. Instead his primary purpose is to assist the individual in the essential process of self-cultivation, so making him fit to take part in government.

The canonization of the text has inevitably resulted in a distortion of its purposes. As I have previously mentioned, the *Analects* is a motley collection of anecdotes and sayings most of which feature Master Kong. Clearly the disciples remembered him for his jokes and irreverences and for his expressions of self-doubt and self-assurance as much as for his profundities. The important content of his teaching, which they presumably continued to purvey, would seem less in need of recording. But commentators and translators have tried to invest all this material with a solemnity which it did not always possess, but which seemed appropriate for the utterances of one who was later regarded as the father of a great tradition. The chapters too are brief and often enigmatic, thus seeming to necessitate extremely tortuous explanations.

Although this is not the place to attempt the tricky enterprise of a thorough survey of the thought underlying the *Analects*, some further information on the content of the work may be gleaned from a reading of the Note on the Translation of Key Terms.

NOTE ON THE TEXT

VARIOUS versions of the *Analects* circulated during the Han Dynasty and it is clear that a work of this name existed even before the Han. The text used in modern times is an eclectic version edited by a scholar who flourished in the first half of the third century AD. In the preparation of this book I have used the text published with the *Analects* volume in the Harvard–Yenching Sinological Index Series. This edition has the advantage that a large number of variant readings is supplied with it. I have proposed no novel emendations and in the few instances where I have used alternative readings my departures from the text are not without precedent so that the reader who understands Chinese will have no difficulty in identifying the version which I have used. Consequently I have provided no list of emendations.

I have followed the division by chapters used in the Harvard–Yenching edition, but the reader who tries to compare my version with others will find that translators have adopted different arrangements, so that sometimes the numbering varies slightly. Despite the editorial work which was lavished on the text in antiquity, the reader will also notice that a few chapters clearly have no connection with the *Analects*, and there are also some repetitions and near repetitions. There is also much material which is either late, alien to the nature of the majority of the work or even hostile to it. For the reader's convenience some such insertions are pointed out in the notes, but by way of generalization it may be stated here that the books whose authenticity one can rely on most confidently are 3–9 and 11–15.

NOTE ON THE TRANSLATION OF
KEY TERMS

BY way of introduction I should say a few words about my
own attitude to translation. I do feel that one should get as
close to the original as possible, even if the result is sometimes a little outlandish. I do not think that it is entirely
virtuous to produce a version which reads as if it were
written at the end of the twentieth century. Some scholars
have been so worried about the difficulty of translating technical terms that they have employed bizarre neologisms,
but I think that it is better to use everyday English words
accompanied by caveats about their meaning. However,
before I deal with specific terms I must say something about
the nature of the language to indicate why translation is so
difficult.

The basic problem is that Classical Chinese is heavily
dependent on context since there is no built-in indication of
whether a word is functioning as a noun, verb, or any other
part of speech. If it is functioning as a verb, there is no
indication of tense or of whether it is being used in the first,
second, or third person or indeed, except in the negative,
whether it is in the indicative or the imperative mood. Moreover, as happens also in other more familiar languages, it is
not possible to tell whether the statement has a general or
particular reference (e.g. does 'the Master did not speak of'
refer to a particular occasion or is it a generalization?). Such
linguistic peculiarities do not cause nearly so much of a
problem as might be expected in normal communication, but
in the brief chapters of the *Analects*, where the material often
lacks context, it is a very different story. This is not entirely
detrimental, however: just as Chinese poetry sometimes
takes on a universal dimension through being couched in a
language which is unspecific about time or person, so too do
chapters of the *Analects* sometimes possess a universal
quality. In such cases I therefore think it a mistake for
translators to introduce person when it is not there by

inserting 'I' or 'you'. It may provide a more accurate reading of the Chinese to make use of the pronoun 'one' if the subject is not made clear by the context. Another difficulty is created by the extremely colloquial nature of the *Analects*. As I have indicated before, it was not written down in solemn philosophical prose. Yet to try to render this with contemporary colloquialisms will seem either ephemeral or overwritten. At the same time there is a rich vocabulary of rare descriptive words and it is impossible to be sure that one has arrived at the best rendering of these.

Having indicated that I have tried to be as close as possible to the original in my translations, I have to confess that there is one respect in which I have introduced modifications in order to try to make things a little easier for the non-specialist reader. Chinese names are notoriously difficult to keep in mind at the best of times, but what adds to the problem is that in the *Analects*, as in some other ancient texts, the same person is referred to by more than one name. Instead of reflecting this practice, which can only result in utter confusion for the non-specialist reader, I have used only one name for each person, with the important exception that I have made use of the personal names which Master Kong used when addressing his disciples, names which could only properly be used by parents or other senior persons. With this one exception I have attempted to get as close to the original as possible, and I certainly do not agree with those who argue that anyone who translates for the non-specialist reader feels constrained to make the material more acceptable at the expense of strict accuracy. Any weaknesses are due either to my own lack of perspicacity or the inadequacy of the English language to convey the Chinese original. These preliminaries having been completed, I can now embark on a discussion of some of the key terms in the *Analects*.

PEOPLE

1. Master (*zi*) is the first word in the *Analects*, in which it occurs many times. *Zi* is also the word which occurs in *junzi* (see (3) below). The original meaning is 'child', as is plain

from the early pictographic form of the character. It occurs as a term of respect and as such it is often a mode of address: 'You, sir'. Often too it occurs in conjunction with the surname of a philosopher, e.g. Kong Zi means 'Master Kong'. Hence, although the word contains no nuance of teacher or philosopher, it has conventionally been translated as 'Master', and this convention has been adopted in this translation as in the great majority of others.

2. Sage (*sheng* or *sheng-ren*, literally 'sage person'). This expression occurs in only six chapters of the *Analects*, although it is much more common in the *Mencius*. In the *Analects* the sage is described as 'someone who benefited the people far and wide and was capable of bringing salvation to the multitude' (6.30). Although this usage does not occur in the *Analects*, the name was later pinned on specific ancient rulers such as the legendary Yao and Shun. *Sheng-ren* were essentially beings of legendary practical wisdom and 'sage' is the generally accepted rendering. This fits the English usage of the term, e.g. when it refers to the seven sages of ancient Greece, who were known for their practical wisdom.

3. Gentleman (*junzi*). The Chinese term literally means 'ruler's son'. It occurs more than a hundred times in the *Analects*. There have been various other translations (e.g. 'the superior man', 'the noble man', 'the exemplary man'), but 'gentleman' is best since it preserves both the original social sense and the ethical sense which develops from it. Although Master Kong was very willing to teach men of ignoble birth and fit them for government, nevertheless it was held that it was the duty of the gentleman in the social sense to behave as a gentleman in the ethical sense, both within the family and within the state. Although in some passages it is not quite clear whether the social or the ethical sense is intended, it is certainly the case that in the great majority of instances *junzi* has become an ethical term.

4. Small man (*xiao ren*). The gentleman is often contrasted with the 'small man', which means a person who is never motivated by moral considerations. In the *Analects* the expression occurs twenty-four times and there is always a specific or implied contrast with *junzi* (gentleman). The literal translation ('small man') has generally been adopted.

5. Men of quality (*xian*) is another general term which occurs in the *Analects*. Whereas 'sage', 'gentleman', and 'small man' play fairly precise roles, *xian* do not have a key function, so translators have not rendered the term consistently, using expressions like 'better', 'superior', 'admirable', 'men of excellence', etc. The general implication is that the *xian* possesses both virtue and ability, so a common rendering is 'men of worth' or 'worthies'. This seems to cover both these aspects, but the word 'worthies' has a slightly condescending nuance to it, so I prefer 'men of quality', whose vagueness fits in with translations like 'better' or 'superior' when the word occurs in comparative contexts. *Xian* also functions as an abstract noun, and in such contexts it is generally rendered by 'merits', 'virtues', or 'excellence', but 'qualities' will serve equally well. Those who are interested in the compilation of the *Analects* may notice that the word occurs only four times in the first half of the book but twenty times in the second half.

6. Three broad categories of official are mentioned as taking part in the government of the state. They are *qing*, *daifu*, and *shi*. The first of these only occurs once and need not detain us since the translation 'minister' is generally accepted. The next in rank, *daifu*, is often rendered 'great officer' and sometimes 'counsellor'. The word literally means 'great person' or 'grand person', and I have generally used the word 'grandee' to give some sense of the meaning, instead of merely reflecting the person's function as the word 'counsellor' does. The third rank, *shi*, is much more difficult to render. It has had various different usages but in imperial times its main meaning was that of scholar–gentleman, i.e. a member of one of the four classes of people into which Chinese society was divided (the other three being agricultural workers, craftsmen, and merchants). The scholar–gentlemen were the class of people who took the civil service examinations and held office. In consequence Legge generally translated the term as 'scholar' or 'officer', but these versions are anachronistic. 'Gentleman' has also been used but this too is inappropriate, especially as it is needed to render *junzi*. At about the time of Master Kong its predominant use seems to have been to describe a class of high-born persons

who had been deprived of their inheritance because of the obliteration of many small states and were now occupied either as military officers or as specialists in the increasingly bureaucratic set-up in the states. As time went on persons of this class did not need to have an aristocratic background. It is very difficult to find a word which will serve in general for all its usages. In the *Analects* the emphasis is clearly not on the specialist tasks which befell the *shi*, but rather on the qualities of character they were supposed to have. Waley used the word 'knight', and I have generally followed suit, with mental inverted commas; but I now feel that it has too many inappropriate resonances and must be abandoned. Hucker in his *Dictionary of Official Titles in Imperial China* uses 'serviceman', which has the wrong flavour (as also has his 'grand master' for *daifu*), so although I like to follow his example, I have not been able to do so in this case. In the end I have preferred 'public servant', which seems to me to have the necessary ethical nuance and also to be usable for administrators throughout the imperial period as well as in the time of Master Kong.

7. The people (*min*). This term is commonly used to refer to the governed. They are almost always depicted as the passive recipients of commands, employment, benefits, instruction, etc. When they are depicted as active, it is only in response to such initiatives by the rulers. Although *min* has generally been translated as 'the people', the word 'masses' has been used, but its political overtones for the modern reader make 'the people' a less objectionable term. Other terms used to mean 'the people' are *zhong* and *bai-xing*. The former is most appropriately rendered 'multitude' and the latter I have translated literally as 'the hundred surnames'. It only occurs in three chapters so it is difficult to be certain, but it is possible that, unlike *min*, it refers to the whole population. Since it referred to people who were grand enough to have surnames, it did not originally allude to every Tom, Dick, and Harry; but by the time of the *Mencius* it had already achieved its modern sense of 'the common people'.

8. People (*ren*). This refers to people as individuals and may sometimes be translated in the singular as 'man' or

'person'. It occurs more than 160 times in the *Analects*, but about half of these usages may be taken as functioning pronominally and may be translated as 'others', or occasionally as 'someone' or 'anyone'. The earliest forms of the character show a drawing of a man.

VIRTUES

9. Humaneness (*ren*). This word is pronounced the same as and is closely related to the above-mentioned *ren* meaning 'man'. It is the key virtue in the *Analects*. It has had a variety of translations, e.g. perfect virtue, kindness, goodness, human-heartedness, benevolence; but it seems to me to be necessary for the version used to render the connection with human beings. The graph consists of 'man' plus 'two' and the word summarizes how a human being should ideally behave towards other human beings, i.e. it embraces all the social virtues. Although it does refer to the individual's attainment of ideal human qualities, it is important not to think of it as merely indicating the psychology of the human being, such as a translation like 'magnanimity' or 'compassion' might suggest. It rather refers to the practical manifestations of being humane. Since it is a supreme and all-embracing virtue, it is not surprising that Master Kong is often depicted as reluctant either to define it or to agree that people have succeeded in achieving it. On the other hand, since the virtue does after all derive from a person's essential humanity, it is sometimes depicted as within easy reach if only one would make the effort to grasp it. Before Master Kong's time the word did not have ethical importance, and its centrality is one of the great innovations of the *Analects*.

10. Virtue (*de*). This is another term with a very general ethical sense. In earlier times it was used to denote a kind of spiritual power or charisma, but in the *Analects* it has already become established as an ethical term. As compared with 'humaneness', 'virtue' (*de*) is a quality which is specifically Heaven-sent. There has been some resistance to using the word 'virtue' because, unlike the English word, it is not used as the opposite of vice, nor is it used as we use it in the

plural as a general term under which separate virtues may be listed. But provided that one remembers that these characteristics are not part of the meaning of the Chinese word *de*, the English word 'virtue' seems to be an adequate translation in the *Analects*. Apart from the ethical sense it is also used to mean 'qualities', just as we may use 'virtues' to describe the qualities of inanimate objects.

11. Loyalty (*zhong*). Some translators have been shy of using 'loyalty' as a translation for *zhong* in the *Analects* because at that early stage it did not imply the blind obedience to superiors which was the appropriate parallel in imperial times to the unswerving filial piety (*xiao*) which sons had to display towards their parents. Indeed it was recognized by James Legge in his translations of the *Analects* and *Mencius* that *zhong* meant 'doing one's best for'. In this sense 'conscientiousness' has sometimes been used as a translation, and this is fairly satisfactory although perhaps too inward-looking. 'Loyalty' does in fact cover the whole range of meanings. Nowadays it is rarely used in the sense of 'blind obedience'. For example, 'a loyal member of a college' means 'one who does his best for the college'. If this is appreciated, it will be understood that the word 'loyalty' will always serve as a satisfactory translation for *zhong*.

12. Filial piety (*xiao*). This term applies to one's attitude both towards living parents and towards dead ancestors. It has obviously been of great importance in China as a result of the central role of ancestor-worship and the importance of the family in Confucian family-centred ethics, but it is mentioned quite rarely in the *Analects*, most of its occurrences coming in the second book. The parallel virtue of dutifulness towards elder brothers (*ti*) is hardly mentioned at all. The word 'piety' is sometimes avoided in translations, 'duty' being used instead; but 'piety' is preferable because it gives the expression a religious flavour and suggests the attitude of reverence which should inform this relationship, a reverence prompted by the knowledge that the parent will eventually become an ancestor and so the object of worship.

13. Good faith (*xin*). This virtue occurs quite often but presents no great problem in interpretation. On several

occasions it is mentioned together with loyalty (*zhong*), and it is seen as the virtue which is particularly appropriate to relationships with friends. It is more than just promise-keeping. It means being utterly truthful in all circumstances. In my translation such alternatives as 'trustworthiness' and 'sincerity' are also included since they sometimes seem more appropriate to the context.

14. Rightness (*yi*). This concept is not discussed or queried in the *Analects*, and the question how one knows that something is right is not posed. The gentleman is concerned with what is right, whereas the small man is concerned with profit. Although an individual is sometimes described as righteous, 'rightness' is normally used to describe acts rather than doers of them, but it is necessary to emphasize that these right acts are not judged in accordance with a set of principles outside oneself which one must learn. The rightness of an act is a consequence of an individual's cumulative experience, and it is against that criterion that it is judged.

15. Other virtues. Two other virtues are considered important although they are hardly mentioned. Reciprocity (*shu*) only occurs twice (and it comes only once in *Mencius*), but it has attracted much attention. It means 'not to impose on others what you yourself do not desire'. There is no single word which satisfactorily renders this into English, so I have persisted with 'reciprocity', although this term is more at home in international law than in ethics. It is obviously an important ingredient in humaneness and in social virtues in general.

Deference (*rang*) is also considered to be a key Confucian virtue although it occurs only half a dozen times in the *Analects* and is even less common in the *Mencius*. It is the virtue shown by Yao and Shun when they abdicated as well as that shown by gentlemen who make way for each other in archery contests. It describes the ceremonious behaviour of the gentleman.

Courage (*yong*) occurs in the sense of either physical or moral courage. Goodness (*shan*) occurs frequently but not primarily as an ethical term. It can be used adjectivally to describe, for example, music, questions, sayings, or adverbially in the sense of 'well' or 'properly'. Often it occurs before a verb in the sense of 'good at' doing something. Although it can be used to describe people, the ethical content is muted or obscure, like 'good' as compared with 'virtuous' or 'righteous' in English. Although the question whether a man is humane (*ren*) is often raised, the question whether a man is good (*shan*) is never asked. When 'good men' are mentioned, the sense seems to be 'competent' or 'efficient' rather than morally good, much the same as 'good' in the 'good at' usage and reminiscent of the verbal use of *shan*, which means 'to consider good', 'to approve'.

TRADITION

Much of the *Analects* is ostensibly concerned with the business of learning from past experience in order to organize the future, and Master Kong is presented as one who is devoted to the task of such transmission. Therefore much is said about:

16. Understanding (*zhi*). This is a broad concept which covers knowledge, awareness, understanding, and appreciation, so I have translated it by any one of these nouns or the related verb. Only the acquisition of knowledge fits one to take part in government and bring about an improvement in society. Great stress is placed on the acquisition of knowledge by:

17. Study/learning (*xue*). These two words have different forces in English: it is possible to study without learning, but it is not possible to learn without study. But the Chinese *xue* covers both. What is made very clear is that *xue* does not necessarily imply the reading of books. One has to learn to be like exemplary persons and learn to deal with moral and political problems. To acquire understanding one obviously needs to study the tradition, which is referred to under the following heads:

18. The Way (*dao*). This term is sometimes used in a specific sense, e.g. the Way of Wen and Wu, the Way of one's father, the Way of the gentleman; but it is generally used without qualification to refer either to the ideal course

of conduct for an individual or to an ideal political organization which once existed and Master Kong ostensibly
hopes will be reintroduced. The emphasis in the *Analects* is
not so much on spelling out the contents of this Way, but
rather on what happens if the Way prevails or does not
prevail in a state. Master Kong is generally depicted as particularly anxious to emphasize that one should not take part
in government unless the Way prevails in a state. If one does,
one's principles are bound to be compromised. The dilemma
is that Master Kong's principles can only be introduced by a
minister entering a corrupt system and reforming it or by a
ruler taking over the Way completely and imposing it.

19. Culture (*wen*). Again the content of culture is not
specified, but it is listed as one of the four subjects (together
with conduct, loyalty, and good faith) taught by the Master
(7.25). Basically the word means 'ornament' or 'decoration'
and is therefore often contrasted with *zhi* meaning 'substance' or 'plain stuff'. In the material world it refers to the
decoration of objects, but in the human world it refers to
all the adornments of civilization, which mark the Chinese
off from the barbarian; so although it may begin with the
decoration on art objects, it develops from that into the
refinements of art and literature. This is what differentiated
China from neighbouring peoples, for civilization (in modern
Chinese *wen-hua* or culture-transformation) meant the
possession of culture, whereas from the Western point of
view civilization originally referred to the institution of cities
as the mark of distinction from more primitive peoples. Thus
King Wen, who laid the foundations for the establishment of
the Zhou Dynasty, was posthumously known as the 'cultured
king'. Culture includes not only literature (the modern
Chinese for which is *wen-xue*, culture study) but also music,
which ideally served as a reflection in sound of a morally
good and beautiful society. Because culture dealt with the
adornments rather than the necessities of life its acquisition
might be thought of as an appropriate use of one's time if
one had any left over from the practice of the social virtues
(cf. 1.6).

20. Ritual (*li*). Originally this referred simply to religious

practice and it generally does so in the *Analects* too; but the attitudes of reverence appropriate to religious ritual are seen as permeating other activities in life, so the word occurs frequently in the *Analects*. Words like *jing*, which is translated as 'reverence' or 'respect', and *gong*, rendered 'courtesy', 'politeness', or 'servility', also occur frequently. In our own times these attitudes may seem less prominent, but they are surely present in all who have marvelled at the wonder of life and of human achievement. One book of the *Analects* (Book 10) is given over entirely to a description of ritual behaviour, and for some Master Kong came to be seen primarily as an expert on the details of ritual (although he would have regarded this as a subject for the specialist rather than the generalist). Later on ritual did take its place alongside music, archery, charioteering, writing, and mathematics as one of the six arts to be acquired by the gentleman, but in the *Analects* its usage is often more general. It is frequently mentioned together with music, the two things both imbuing and reflecting the ideal society.

21. Heaven (*tian*). Although there is much in the *Analects* about the observance of ritual both in religious and secular contexts, the work does not include specifically religious teaching and Master Kong is depicted as displaying an agnostic attitude towards ghosts and spirits, although they are seen as part of the general experience of life. On the other hand he is very conscious of the role of Heaven who 'created the virtue' in him, and upon whom all riches and honours depend, while others are described in the *Analects* as believing that Heaven is using the Master and will grant that he becomes a sage. A more impersonal 'fate' or 'destiny' (*ming*), a word which is also used in its more literal sense of 'decree' or 'command', also occurs commonly. It reflects the feeling which must be common to all cultures that, despite all our efforts, what happens is really out of our hands (although commands and decrees can of course be disobeyed and one can, for example, lay down one's life and so not accept one's predestined span). The combination of the two words to make 'decree of Heaven' (*tian-ming*) only occurs twice in passages which may be unauthentic and certainly do

not bear the sense of the later usage, in which the 'Mandate of Heaven' is a guarantee of the legitimacy of the government. Indeed in interpreting this term, as in dealing with others one should always bear in mind the nature of the *Analects*, which is itself a warning not to expect consistency in the treatment of topics.

This note has devoted much space to elucidating my translation of certain important terms, but I must finally emphasize the difficulty which exists in reaching decisions about the most appropriate English version to use. All writers of English carry around a heavy baggage of preconceptions which derive ultimately from Western philosophical and religious beliefs. In translating from a cultural sphere which does not share these prejudices and from a language whose very nature may to some extent impose its own world-view we are, however, bound to use terms which depend heavily upon Western traditions. In short, translation—at least of philosophical works—can at best only be an approximation. That does not mean that we should shrug our shoulders pharisaically and accept the argument of those who believe that only a translation with full critical apparatus and exhaustive notes can advance the cause of knowledge. It is true that it is in the art of interpreting this material for the specialist reader that the fun of scholarship really begins. It is nevertheless sad that, in the arts as well as in the sciences, academic communication increasingly consists of professionals writing for their fellow professionals: this cannot be helpful to the long-term prosperity of scholarship, and in a shrinking world it would be particularly tragic if specialists in ancient cultures totally failed to communicate with the wider public. In any case I believe that we should not always be trying to preach to the converted, but should do our best to try to achieve a piece of inter-cultural communication and make the *Analects* as intelligible as possible to people of our own culture.

NOTE ON ROMANIZATION

PINYIN is the official romanization system of the People's Republic of China and is in common use outside China not only for works of scholarship but also for use in the media. Although it has largely replaced the Wade–Giles system, since no other translations of the *Analects* apart from this one employ *pinyin* and much important writing on Chinese philosophy has employed Wade–Giles, I now append a conversion table between *pinyin* and Wade–Giles, omitting all the sounds, amounting to approximately one-third of the total number, which are written the same in the two romanizations.

Before I do so a few preliminary words may help with the pronunciation. In *pinyin* the consonants sound approximately as written, except that 'q' sounds like English 'ch', 'c' sounds like English 'ts', and 'x' sounds rather like English 'sh'. Readers may also find 'zh' puzzling, e.g. in 'Zhou'. That is what sounds like the English Christian name 'Joe' and is written 'Chou' in Wade–Giles. The vowel-sounds require more tuition than a book of this nature would justify, but it might be useful to know that the furthest departure from English usages are that 'e' is pronounced rather like the 'ir' in 'sir', except after 'i' and 'y' when it is pronounced as in the English 'yes'; and that 'i', although normally like the 'ee' in 'bee', is a cross between 'ir' in 'sir' and 'oo' in 'good', when it occurs in 'chi', 'ri', 'shi', and 'zhi'.

Pinyin	Wade–Giles	Pinyin	Wade–Giles
ba	pa	beng	peng
bai	pai	bi	pi
ban	pan	bian	pien
bang	pang	biao	piao
bao	pao	bie	pieh
bei	pei	bin	pin
ben	pen	bing	ping

Pinyin	Wade–Giles	Pinyin	Wade–Giles
bo	po	cun	ts'un
bou	pou	cuo	ts'o
bu	pu		
		da	ta
ca	ts'a	dai	tai
cai	ts'ai	dan	tan
can	ts'an	dang	tang
cang	ts'ang	dao	tao
cao	ts'ao	de	te
ce	ts'e	deng	teng
cen	ts'en	di	ti
ceng	ts'eng	dian	tien
cha	ch'a	diao	tiao
chai	ch'ai	die	tieh
chan	ch'an	ding	ting
chang	ch'ang	diu	tiu
chao	ch'ao	dong	tung
che	ch'e	dou	tou
chen	ch'en	du	tu
cheng	ch'eng	duan	tuan
chi	ch'ih	dui	tui
chong	ch'ung	dun	tun
chou	ch'ou	duo	to
chu	ch'u		
chua	ch'ua	e	o
chuai	ch'uai	er	erh
chuan	ch'uan		
chuang	ch'uang	ga	ka
chui	ch'ui	gai	kai
chun	ch'un	gan	kan
chuo	ch'o	gang	kang
ci	tz'u	gao	kao
cong	ts'ung	ge	ko
cou	ts'ou	gei	kei
cu	ts'u	gen	ken
cuan	ts'uan	geng	keng
cui	ts'ui	gong	kung

Pinyin	Wade–Giles	Pinyin	Wade–Giles
gou	kou	kong	k'ung
gu	ku	kou	k'ou
gua	kua	ku	k'u
guai	kuai	kua	k'ua
guan	kuan	kuai	k'uai
guang	kuang	kuan	k'uan
gui	kuei	kuang	k'uang
gun	kun	kui	k'uei
guo	kuo	kun	k'un
		kuo	k'uo
he	ho		
hong	hung	lian	lien
		lie	lieh
ji	chi	long	lung
jia	chia	lue	lüeh
jian	chien	luo	lo
jiang	chiang		
jiao	chiao	mian	mien
jie	chieh	mie	mieh
jin	chin		
jing	ching	nian	nien
jiong	chiung	nie	nieh
jiu	chiu	nong	nung
ju	chü	nue	nüeh
juan	chüan		
jue	chüeh	pa	p'a
jun	chün	pai	p'ai
		pan	p'an
ka	k'a	pang	p'ang
kai	k'ai	pao	p'ao
kan	k'an	pei	p'ei
kang	k'ang	pen	p'en
kao	k'ao	peng	p'eng
ke	k'o	pi	p'i
kei	k'ei	pian	p'ien
ken	k'en	piao	p'iao
keng	k'eng	pie	p'ieh

Pinyin	Wade–Giles	Pinyin	Wade–Giles
pin	p'in	si	ssu
ping	p'ing	song	sung
po	p'o	suo	so
pou	p'ou		
pu	p'u	ta	t'a
		tai	t'ai
qi	ch'i	tan	t'an
qia	ch'ia	tang	t'ang
qian	ch'ien	tao	t'ao
qiang	ch'iang	te	t'e
qiao	ch'iao	teng	t'eng
qie	ch'ieh	ti	t'i
qin	ch'in	tian	t'ien
qing	ch'ing	tiao	t'iao
qiong	ch'iung	tie	t'ieh
qiu	ch'iu	ting	t'ing
qu	ch'ü	tong	t'ung
quan	ch'üan	tou	t'ou
que	ch'üeh	tu	t'u
qun	ch'ün	tuan	t'uan
		tui	t'ui
ran	jan	tun	t'un
rang	jang	tuo	t'o
rao	jao		
re	je	xi	hsi
ren	jen	xia	hsia
reng	jeng	xian	hsien
ri	jih	xiang	hsiang
rong	jung	xiao	hsiao
rou	jou	xie	hsieh
ru	ju	xin	hsin
ruan	juan	xing	hsing
rui	jui	xiong	hsiung
run	jun	xiu	hsiu
ruo	jo	xu	hsü
		xuan	hsüan
shi	shih	xue	hsüeh

Pinyin	Wade–Giles	Pinyin	Wade–Giles
xun	hsün	zhang	chang
		zhao	chao
yan	yen	zhe	che
ye	yeh	zhen	chen
yi	i	zheng	cheng
yong	yung	zhi	chih
you	yu	zhong	chung
yu	yü	zhou	chou
yuan	yüan	zhu	chu
yue	yüeh	zhua	chua
yun	yün	zhuai	chuai
		zhuan	chuan
za	tsa	zhuang	chuang
zai	tsai	zhui	chui
zan	tsan	zhun	chun
zang	tsang	zhuo	cho
zao	tsao	zi	tzu
ze	tse	zong	tsung
zei	tsei	zou	tsou
zen	tsen	zu	tsu
zeng	tseng	zuan	tsuan
zha	cha	zui	tsui
zhai	chai	zun	tsun
zhan	chan	zuo	tso

SELECT BIBLIOGRAPHY

THOSE who wish to delve more deeply into the *Analects* should look at D. C. Lau's *Confucius: The Analects* (Harmondsworth, 1979). Although they will find the explanatory notes too brief, there is a valuable introduction on the philosophy and useful appendices on the life of Confucius, the disciples, and the compilation of the *Analects*. The other English versions still regarded as useful are those by James Legge and Arthur Waley. The former's translation (first published in Hong Kong in 1861 as volume 1 of his *The Chinese Classics*) has the advantage of including the original text and detailed commentary, but he was under the influence of orthodox Chinese attitudes and his missionary approach to the essentially humanist philosophy of Confucius is inevitably misleading. Although Arthur Waley was a magnificent interpreter of Chinese literature to the West, *The Analects of Confucius* (London, 1938) was regarded by its author as 'somewhat dry and technical in character'; and it is certainly true that many of his explanatory notes are unintelligible unless the reader knows Chinese. Possibly the most useful version for the non-specialist reader is P. Ryckmans's French translation (*Les Entretiens de Confucius*, Paris, 1987), which includes long notes on some of the points which require explanation. My own short book *Confucius* (Oxford, 1981) is also designed for nonspecialist readers. It groups important chapters of the *Analects* under topical headings and stresses its importance as a seminal statement of Chinese attitudes. (The percipient reader will notice slight changes of interpretation in the present volume. I hope this indicates progress.)

On the historical background it is necessary to look at the relevant section of one of the general histories of China, such as J. Gernet's *A History of Chinese Civilization* (Cambridge, 1982). B. I. Schwarz's *The World of Thought in Ancient China* (Cambridge, Mass., 1985) is an excellent introduction to ancient Chinese philosophy by a distinguished scholar, while Wing-tsit Chan's *A Source Book in Chinese Philosophy* (Princeton, NJ, and Oxford, 1963) is a useful collection of translations. Some sophisticated work has recently been done on the philosophy of the *Analects*, some of it appearing in periodicals such as *Philosophy East and West* and the *Journal of Chinese Philosophy*. The reader may also come across important books like H. Fingarette's *Confucius: The Secular as Sacred* (New

York, 1972), and D. L. Hall and R. T. Ames's *Thinking Through Confucius* (New York, 1987), but should be warned that they are difficult for the non-specialist reader to appreciate and also have not met with the universal approval of specialists.

CHRONOLOGICAL SURVEY

THIS survey is not restricted to the *Analects*, but also covers important people and events in the history of Confucianism.

3rd mill. BC	Age of the legendary sage-kings Yao, Shun, and Yu.
legendary	Xia Dynasty, founded by sage-king Yu.
c.1525–1025	Yin Dynasty, also known as Shang.
c.1025–256	Zhou Dynasty (founded by King Wu after King Wen had laid the cultural foundations). Wu was succeeded by his son Cheng, with Duke of Zhou acting as regent for part of reign.
680	Duke Huan (who reigned over Qi from 685 to 643) becomes first head of alliance of northern Chinese states including Master Kong's state of Lu.
632	Duke Wen (who reigned over Jin from 636 to 628) is second head of this alliance.
551	Traditional date of Master Kong's birth.
541–509	Lu reigned over by Duke Zhao.
509–495	Lu reigned over by Duke Ding.
497–484	Master Kong travelling in other Chinese states.
494–468	Lu reigned over by Duke Ai, but as in the previous reign real power in the hands of the Three Families, especially the Ji.
479	Traditional date of Master Kong's death.
c.370–290	Master Meng (Mencius), the most famous follower of Master Kong.
221	State of Qin unifies China.
213	Burning of Books.
206	Qin Dynasty replaced by Han Dynasty.
140–87	Reign of Emperor Wu.
124	Foundation of imperial academy.
589	Sui Dynasty reunites China.
606	Recruitment examinations resumed.
960	Start of Song Dynasty, when Confucian texts began to dominate examinations.
1905	Abolition of examinations based on Confucian texts.

The Analects

1. The Master said: 'To learn something and at times to practise it—surely that is a pleasure? To have friends coming from distant places—surely that is delightful? But not to be resentful at others' failure to appreciate one—surely that is to be a true gentleman?'

2. Master You* said: 'Few indeed are those who are naturally filial towards their parents and dutiful towards their elder brothers but are fond of opposing their superiors; and it never happens that those who do not like opposing their superiors are fond of creating civil disorder.* The gentleman concerns himself with the root; and if the root is firmly planted, the Way grows. Filial piety and fraternal duty—surely they are the roots of humaneness.'

3. The Master said: 'Clever words and a plausible appearance have seldom turned out to be humane.'

4. Master Zeng* said: 'Every day I examine my character in three respects: am I disloyal in my designs for others, am I untrustworthy in my dealings with friends, have I failed to practise what has been passed on to me?'

5. The Master said: 'In leading a country of a thousand chariots* one deals reverently with the business and exercises good faith, one is economical in expenditure* and displays love of others, and one employs the people only in due season.'

6. The Master said: 'Young men should be filial when at home and respectful to elders when away from home. They should be earnest and trustworthy. Although they should love the multitude far and wide, they should be intimate only with the humane. If they have any energy to spare after so doing, they should use it to study "culture".'

7. Zixia* said: 'If he appreciates men of quality, if he makes light of sexual attraction, if in serving his father and mother he is capable of using his strength to the utmost, if in serving his lord he is capable of offering up his life, if in his dealings with friends he is trustworthy in what he says, I

would certainly call him learned even if it is said that he has never studied.'

8.   The Master said: 'If the gentleman is not grave, then he does not inspire awe. If he studies, then he is not inflexible. He takes loyalty and good faith as his first principles, and has no friends who are not up to his own standard. If he commits a fault, he should not shrink from correcting it.'

9.   Master Zeng said: 'Show solicitude for parents at the end of their lives and continue this with sacrifices when they are far away, and the people's virtue will be restored to fullness.'

10.   Ziqin asked Zigong:* 'When our Master arrives at a certain country, he always hears about its government. Does he seek this information or do they give it to him?' Zigong said: 'The Master is warm, amiable, courteous, frugal, and deferential, and through these qualities he obtains the information. Surely the Master's method of seeking it is different from the way other men seek it?'

11.   The Master said: 'When his father is alive, you observe a man's intentions. It is when the father is dead that you observe the man's actions. If for three years he makes no change from the ways of his father, he may be called filial.'*

12.   Master You said: 'In the practice of the rites harmony is regarded as the most valuable thing, and in the ways of the ancient kings this is regarded as the most beautiful thing. It is adopted in all matters, both small and great. But sometimes it does not work. If you behave harmoniously because you understand harmony, but do not regulate your conduct with ritual,* surely that cannot be made to work.'

13.   Master You said: 'When good faith is close to righteousness, one's words may be fulfilled. When courtesy is close to the rites, one keeps shame and dishonour at a distance. If in marriage one does not bring loss to one's relatives, one is surely fit to be honoured as head of the clan.'

14.   The Master said: 'A gentleman avoids seeking to satisfy his appetite to the full when he eats and avoids seeking comfort when he is at home. He is diligent in deed and cautious in word, and he associates with possessors of the

Way and is put right by them. He may simply be said to be fond of learning.'

15. Zigong said: ' "Poor but avoiding obsequiousness, rich but avoiding arrogance"—what about that?' The Master said: 'That will do, but it is not at all as good as "Poor but delighting in the Way,* rich but loving ritual".' Zigong said: 'The *Songs** say: "As cut, as filed, as chiselled, as polished." Presumably this applies to what you have just said?' The Master said: 'As far as Si* is concerned, now it is definitely possible to talk about the *Songs* with him: if I report what has already occurred, he knows what is to come.'

16. The Master said: 'One does not worry about the fact that other people do not appreciate one. One worries about not appreciating other people.'

BOOK 2

Way asserts that right by them. He may simply be said to be
fond of learning.

15. Zigong said: 'Poor but avoiding obsequiousness, rich
but avoiding arrogance – what about that?' The Master

1. The Master said: 'The practice of government by means
of virtue may be compared with the pole-star,* which the
multitudinous stars pay homage to while it stays in its place.'

2. The Master said: 'The *Songs* number three hundred, but
I will cover their meaning with a single quotation: "Let there
be no depravity in your thoughts."'*

3. The Master said: 'If you lead them by means of government and keep order among them by means of punishments,
the people are without conscience in evading them. If you
lead them by means of virtue and keep order among them by
means of ritual, they have a conscience and moreover will
submit.'

4. The Master said: 'At fifteen I set my heart on learning, at
thirty I was established, at forty I had no perplexities, at fifty
I understood the decrees of Heaven, at sixty my ear was in
accord, and at seventy* I followed what my heart desired but
did not transgress what was right.'

5. Meng Yi Zi* asked about filial piety and the Master
said: 'Avoid breaking the rules.' When he was being driven
by Fan Chi, the Master told him: 'Meng asked me about
filial piety and I replied saying: "Avoid breaking the rules."'
Fan Chi said: 'What did you mean?' The Master said: 'When
you serve them while they are alive do so in accordance with
the rites; and after they are dead, when you bury them, do so
in accordance with the rites and, when you sacrifice to them,
do so in accordance with the rites.'

6. Meng Wu Bo asked about filial piety and the Master
said: 'It is when father's and mother's only worry is about
one being ill.'

7. Ziyou* asked about filial piety. The Master said: 'As far
as present-day filial piety is concerned, this means being able
to provide sustinence; but even dogs and horses are all able
to receive sustinence. If reverence is not shown, how does
one tell the difference?'

8. Zixia asked about filial piety. The Master said: 'It is the

demeanour that is difficult. If the young people bear the brunt of their elders' labours when there is work to be done, and if the elders are provided with sustinence when there is wine and food available, then does one consider that this constitutes filial piety?'

9. The Master said: 'I spend the whole day talking with Hui,* and he does not put any counter-arguments but seems stupid; but when he is no longer with me and I study his private conduct, he is after all capable of setting an example. Hui is certainly not stupid.'

10. The Master said: 'See how he operates, observe what path he follows, examine what he is satisfied with, and how can a man remain inscrutable, how can a man remain inscrutable!'

11. The Master said: 'If by keeping the old warm one can provide understanding of the new, one is fit to be a teacher.'

12. The Master said: 'A gentleman does not behave as an implement.'*

13. Zigong asked about the gentleman. The Master said: 'He puts his sayings into action before adopting them as guidelines.'

14. The Master said: 'The gentleman has universal sympathies and is not partisan. The small man is partisan and does not have universal sympathies.'

15. The Master said: 'If one studies but does not think, one is caught in a trap. If one thinks but does not study, one is in peril.'

16. * The Master said: 'If one is attacked from different starting points, it is indeed damaging.'

17. The Master said: 'You,* shall I teach you about understanding something? When you understand something, to recognize that you understand it; but when you do not understand something, to recognize that you do not understand it—that is understanding.'

18. Zizhang was studying with an official career in view. The Master said: 'If you hear much but omit doubtful points and speak cautiously about the rest of it, then you will seldom be to blame. If you see much but omit what is dangerous and cautiously put into practice the rest of it, then

you will seldom feel regret. If your words are seldom blamed and your actions are seldom regretted, then an official career will be open to you.'

19. Duke Ai* asked: 'What action does one take so that the people will be obedient?' Master Kong replied saying: 'If you promote the straight and set them above the crooked, then the people will be obedient. If you promote the crooked and set them above the straight, then the people will not be obedient.'

20. Ji Kang Zi* asked how the people might be induced to be respectful and loyal so that they might be properly encouraged. The Master said: 'If you oversee them with dignity, they will be respectful. If you are dutiful towards your parents and kind to your children, then they will be loyal. If you promote the good and instruct the incompetent, then they will be encouraged.'

21. Someone said to Master Kong: 'Why do you not take part in government?' The Master said: 'The *Book of Documents** mentions filial piety, doesn't it? "Only be dutiful towards your parents and friendly towards your brothers, and you will be contributing to the existence of government." These virtues surely constitute taking part in government, so why should only that particular activity be regarded as taking part in government?'

22. The Master said: 'If someone is untrustworthy in spite of being a man, I do not know that he will do. If carriages have no means of yoking horses* to them, how are they ever made to go?'

23. Zizhang asked whether ten generations hence could be known about. The Master said: 'The Yin* based itself on the Xia ritual and what they subtracted or added may be known. The Zhou based itself on the Yin ritual and what they subtracted or added may be known. The Zhou's possible successors even in a hundred generations may be known about.'

24. The Master said: 'To sacrifice to the spirits of ancestors who are not one's own is obsequiousness, and to see what is right and not do it is cowardice.'

BOOK 3

1. Master Kong said: 'The Ji family has eight rows of dancers* performing in the courtyard. If this can be endured, what cannot be endured?'
2. The Three Families cleared the sacrificial vessels accompanied by the *Yong*.* The Master said:

> '"In attendance are the lords and princes.
> The Son of Heaven is awesome and majestic."

What has this got to do with the halls of the Three Families?'
3. The Master said: 'If someone is not humane in spite of being a man, what has he to do with ritual? If someone is not humane in spite of being a man, what has he to do with music?'
4. Lin Fang asked about the root of ritual. The Master said: 'An important question indeed! In ritual it is better to be frugal rather than lavish, but in mourning it is better to be sorrowful rather than unmoved.'
5. The Master said: 'Barbarian peoples with rulers are not as good as the various Chinese states without them.'
6. The Ji family was sacrificing to Mount Tai. The Master said to Ran You:* 'Can you not go to their rescue?' 'I cannot', he replied. 'Alas and alack!' said the Master. 'Then do you mean that Mount Tai is not as good as Lin Fang?'
7. The Master said: 'There is nothing which gentlemen compete over. If competition were inevitable, it would be in archery, wouldn't it? But they go up, bowing and making way for each other; and when they come down, they have a drink. So even in their competition with each other, they are gentlemen.'
8. Zixia asked the meaning of the lines:

> The entrancing smile dimpling,
> The beautiful eyes shining,
> Plain silk which is made into finery.*

The Master said: 'The decoration comes after the plain silk.'
'Is ritual secondary?' he said. 'Shang is the one who takes my
point', said the Master. 'Now it is definitely possible to talk
about the *Songs* with him.'

9.   The Master said: 'The Xia ritual I can talk about
although Qi* is not worth taking as evidence. The Yin ritual
I can talk about although Song is not worth taking as evidence. This is because both the documents and the men of
learning are not adequate to be taken as a basis. If they were
adequate, then I could take them as evidence.'

10.   The Master said: 'At the *di* sacrifice* I do not wish to
witness what comes after the libation.'

11.   Someone enquired about the meaning of the *di* sacrifice.
'This is something I do not understand', said the Master.
'The relationship to all under Heaven of one who did understand its meaning would be like putting this here.' And he
put his finger on the palm of his hand.

12.   'Sacrifice as if present'* means 'Sacrifice to the spirits as
if the *spirits* were in one's presence'; but the Master said: 'If
I myself do not take part in a sacrifice, it is as if no sacrifice
is made.'

13.   Wangsun Jia asked: 'What is the meaning of

> "Better to fawn on the stove
> Than to fawn on the south-west corner"?'*

The Master said: 'It is not so. If you offend against Heaven,
there is no one to pray to.'

14.   The Master said: 'Zhou observes the example set by
two dynasties, so how splendid is its culture! And we take
Zhou as our model.'

15.   When the Master entered the grand temple,* he asked
about every single thing. Someone said: 'Who says that the
son of the man from Zou knows the ritual? When he enters
the grand temple, he asks about every single thing.' When the
Master heard this, he said: 'This is the ritual.'

16.   The Master said: 'In archery it was the Way of antiquity
not to stress the leather,* because strength is not evenly
matched.'

17.   Zigong wished to do away with the sacrificial sheep at

the announcement of the new moon. The Master said: 'Si, you begrudge the sheep used in this, but I begrudge the ritual involved in it.'

18. The Master said: 'The full observance of ritual in serving a ruler is regarded by others as sycophancy.'

19. Duke Ding* asked how rulers should employ ministers, and how ministers should serve rulers. Master Kong replied: 'Rulers in employing ministers do so in accordance with ritual, and ministers in serving rulers do so in accordance with loyalty.'

20. The Master said: 'In the *Guan ju** they are joyful but not wanton, they suffer grief but are not harmed.'

21. Duke Ai asked Zai Wo* about the altar to the earth god. Zai Wo replied saying: 'The Xia used the pine, the men of Yin used the cypress, and the men of Zhou used the chestnut, saying that it would make the people tremble.'* When the Master heard this, he said: 'What is over and done with one does not discuss, what has taken its course one does not complain about, and what is already past one does not criticize.'

22. The Master said: 'Guan Zhong's capacity was small indeed.' Someone said: 'Guan Zhong* was thrifty, was he?' He said: 'Guan Zhong kept three establishments, and in his official business he did not take over other people's duties, so how does he get a reputation for thrift?' 'Nevertheless Guan Zhong did understand the rites, didn't he?' He said: 'Rulers of states erect gate-screens, and Guan also erected a gate-screen; rulers of states, when they held a friendly meeting with another ruler, had a stand for inverted cups, and Guan also had a stand for inverted cups. If even Guan Zhong understood the rites, who does not understand the rites?'

23. The Master talked about music to the Grand Music-master of Lu saying: 'Their music, insofar as it may be known about, tended to be in unison when they started to play. Following upon this, it was somewhat harmonious, clear, and unbroken right through until it was finished.'

24. The boundaryman at Yi requested to be presented, saying: 'When gentlemen come here, I have never failed to get presented.' The followers presented him, and as he came

out, he said: 'What have you gentlemen to be disheartened at in his failure? It is a long time since the Way prevailed in the world, but Heaven is about to use your Master as a wooden warning-bell.'

25. The Master said that the *shao** was perfectly beautiful and also perfectly good. He said of the *wu* that it was perfectly beautiful, but not perfectly good.'

26. The Master said: 'Intolerance when occupying a high position, irreverence when performing ritual, and being unsorrowful in the conduct of mourning—how am I to contemplate these things?'

BOOK 4

1. The Master said: 'It is humaneness which is the attraction of a neighbourhood.* If from choice one does not dwell in humaneness, how does one obtain wisdom?'

2. The Master said: 'It is impossible for those who are not humane to dwell for a long time in adversity, and it is also impossible for them to dwell for long in pleasurable circumstances. Those who are humane rest content with humaneness and those who are wise derive advantage from humaneness.'

3. The Master said: 'Only one who is humane is able to like other people and able to dislike other people.'

4. The Master said: 'If one sets one's heart on humaneness, one will be without evil.'

5. The Master said: 'Riches and honours—these are what men desire, but if this is not achieved in accordance with the appropriate principles, one does not cling to them. Poverty and obscurity—these are what men hate, but if this is not achieved in accordance with the appropriate principles, one does not avoid them. If a gentleman abandons humaneness, how does he make a reputation? The gentleman never shuns humaneness even for the time it takes to finish a meal. If his progress is hasty, it is bound to arise from this; and if his progress is unsteady, it is bound to arise from this.'

6. The Master said: 'I have never come across anyone who loved humaneness and hated inhumaneness. As far as anyone who loved humaneness is concerned, there would be no way of surpassing him. As far as anyone who hated inhumaneness is concerned, in his practice of humaneness he would not let the inhumane come near his person. Does there exist anyone who is capable of devoting his energies to humaneness for a single day? I have never come across anyone whose energies were inadequate. Surely such people exist, but I have never come across them.'

7. The Master said: 'People's mistakes all come in the same

category in that, if one contemplates a mistake, then one gains an understanding of humaneness.'

8. The Master said: 'If one has heard the Way in the morning, it is all right to die in the evening.'

9. The Master said: 'A public servant who is intent on the Way, but is ashamed of bad clothes and bad food, is not at all fit to be consulted.'

10. The Master said: 'In his attitude to the world the gentleman has no antagonisms and no favouritisms. What is right he sides with.'

11. The Master said: 'The gentleman cherishes virtue, but the small man cherishes the soil; the gentleman cherishes the rigours of the law, but the small man cherishes leniency.'

12. The Master said: 'If one acts with a view to profit, there will be much resentment.'

13. The Master said: 'If one can run a country by making use of the deferential attitudes induced by ritual, what difficulty will there be? But if one cannot run a country by making use of the deferential attitudes induced by ritual, then what point is there in ritual?'

14. The Master said: 'One is not worried about not holding position; one is worried about how one may fit oneself for appointment. One is not worried that nobody knows one; one seeks to become fit to be known.'

15. The Master said: 'Can, by one single thread is my Way bound together.' Master Zeng said: 'Yes.' When the Master went out the disciples asked: 'What did he mean?' Master Zeng said: 'Our Master's Way simply consists of loyalty and reciprocity.'

16. The Master said: 'The gentleman is familiar with what is right, just as the small man is familiar with profit.'

17. The Master said: 'When you come across a superior person, think of being equal to him. When you come across an inferior person, turn inwards and examine yourself.'

18. The Master said: 'In serving father and mother, one remonstrates gently. If one sees that they are intent on not following advice, one continues to be respectful and does not show disobedience; and even if one finds it burdensome, one does not feel resentful.'

19.　The Master said: 'When father and mother are alive, one does not travel far; and if one does travel, one must have a fixed destination.'*

20.　The Master said: 'If for three years one makes no change from the ways of one's father, one may be called filial.'

21.　The Master said: 'The age of one's father and mother should not be unknown, on the one hand so that one may rejoice, and on the other hand so that one may feel anxiety.'

22.　The Master said: 'The reason why words were not readily uttered in antiquity was because people were ashamed that they personally would not come up to them.'

23.　The Master said: 'There are few indeed who fail in something through exercising restraint.'

24.　The Master said: 'The gentleman wishes to be slow in speech but prompt in action.'

25.　The Master said: 'Virtue is not solitary. It is bound to have neighbours.'

26.　Ziyou said: 'If one is censorious when serving one's ruler, then one falls into disgrace; but if one is censorious with one's friends, then one becomes estranged.'

1. The Master said of Gongye Chang that he might be given a wife for, although he had been put in prison, this was not through any crime of his. He gave him his own daughter in marriage.

2. The Master said of Nan Rong that if the Way prevailed in a state, he would not be discarded; and, if the Way did not prevail in a state, he would avoid punishment and humiliation. He gave him the daughter of his elder brother in marriage.

3. The Master said of Zijian: 'A gentleman indeed is such as he. If there had been no gentlemen in Lu, then where would he have got this from?'

4. Zigong asked: 'What sort of person am I?' The Master said: 'You are a vessel.' He said: 'What sort of vessel?' The reply was 'A jade sacrificial vessel.'*

5. Someone said: 'Although Yong* is humane, he is not eloquent.' The Master said: 'What is the point of eloquence? Those who confront others with a ready tongue are often hated by them. I do not know about his being humane, but what is the point of eloquence?'

6. The Master charged Qidiao Kai to take an official position, but he replied saying: 'This I am not yet capable of fulfilling in a trustworthy manner.' The Master was pleased.

7. The Master said: 'If the Way is not practised and I float out to sea travelling on a raft,* the one who accompanies me will be You, won't it?' When Zilu heard this, he was delighted. The Master said: 'You is the sort of person who surpasses me in love of courage, but there is no point in his having acquired such talents.'

8. Meng Wu Bo asked whether Zilu was humane. The Master said: 'It is not known.' He asked again and the Master said: 'He could be employed to organize military levies in a country of a thousand chariots, but I do not know that he is humane.' 'What about Qiu?'* The Master said: 'Qiu could be employed as steward for a city of a thousand

households or a family with a hundred chariots, but I do not know that he is humane.' 'What about Chi?'* The Master said: 'Chi, if he puts on his sash and takes his place at court, may be employed to converse with the guests, but I do not know that he is humane.'

9. The Master said to Zigong: 'Out of You and Hui which is the better?' He replied: 'How dare I even have a look at Hui? Hui is the sort of person who, by hearing one thing, understands ten; but I am the sort of person who, by hearing one thing, understands two.' The Master said: 'You are not as good as he is. Both you and I are not as good as he is.'

10. Zai Wo was in bed during the daytime. The Master said: 'Rotten wood cannot be carved and a dirt wall cannot be trowelled. In Yu what is to be punished?' The Master went on: 'First of all when I dealt with people, having listened to their words, I took their deeds on trust; but now, when I deal with people, having listened to their words, I observe their deeds. It is because of Yu that I have made this change.'

11. The Master said: 'I have never come across anyone who is unyielding.' Someone replied: 'Shen Cheng.' The Master said: 'Cheng is lustful, so how can he be unyielding?'

12. Zigong said: 'If I do not want others to inflict something on me, I also want to avoid inflicting it on others.' The Master said: 'Si, this is not a point you have yet reached.'

13. Zigong said: 'The Master's accomplishments one can get to hear about, but what he has to say about human nature and the way of Heaven* one cannot get to hear about.'

14. If there was something Zilu had heard, but he had not yet been able to put it into practice, his only fear was of hearing something else.

15. Zigong asked why they called Kong Wen Zi 'cultured' (*wen*). The Master said: 'He was diligent and fond of learning, and he was not ashamed to ask questions of those beneath him. That is why they called him "cultured".'

16. The Master said that there were four of the ways of the gentleman present in Zichan:* in his conduct of himself he was courteous, in his service of his superiors he showed veneration, in his provision for the needs of the people he

was generous, and in his employment of the people he was righteous.

17. The Master said: 'Yan Pingzhong* was good at relationships with others: even over a long period he showed respect for them.'

18. The Master said: 'Zang Wenzhong* housed a giant tortoise, with hills carved on the capitals of the pillars of its dwelling and duckweed carved on the rafterposts. What sort of understanding was his?'

19. Zizhang asked saying: 'Chief Minister Ziwen* three times held office as chief minister, but showed no sign of delight; three times he was deposed, but showed no sign of resentment. He always reported to the new chief minister on the conduct of government of himself, the former chief minister. So what do you think of him?' The Master said: 'He was loyal.' 'Was he humane?' said Zizhang. 'I do not yet understand', said the Master, 'how he could be considered humane.' Zizhang said: 'When Cui Zi assassinated the Lord of Qi, Chen Wen Zi, although he owned ten teams of horses, abandoned them and left the place. When he reached another country, he said: "They are no different from our grandee Cui Zi", and left the place. When he came to another country, he again said: "They are no different from our grandee Cui Zi", and left the place. So what do you think of him?' The Master said: 'He was pure.' 'Was he humane?' said Zizhang. 'I do not yet understand', said the Master, 'how he could be considered humane.'

20. Ji Wen Zi thought three times before acting. When the Master heard of this, he said: 'Twice will do.'*

21. The Master said: 'When the Way prevailed in the state, Ning Wu Zi was wise, but when the Way did not prevail in the state, he was stupid. His wisdom is attainable, but his stupidity is unattainable.'

22. When the Master was in Chen, he said: 'Shall I go back, shall I go back! The young men of my locality are headstrong and careless. They have brilliantly perfected their accomplishments, but do not know how to tailor them.'

23. The Master said: 'Bo Yi and Shu Qi* did not remember

old ills and hence feelings of resentment towards them were rare.'

24. The Master said: 'Who says that Weisheng Gao* was upright? Someone begged vinegar from him and he begged it from his neighbour and handed it over.'

25. The Master said: 'Clever words, a plausible appearance, and excessive courtesy—Zuoqiu Ming found them shameful, and I too find them shameful. Concealing resentment and befriending the person towards whom one feels resentful—Zuoqiu Ming found this shameful, and I too find this shameful.'

26. Yan Hui and Zilu were in attendance. The Master said: 'Why do you not each express your aspirations?' Zilu said: 'I should like to share my carriage and horses, clothing* and furs with my friends and feel no annoyance if they wear them out.' Yan Hui said: 'I should like not to boast of my excellence and not to show off my hard work.' Zilu said: 'I should like to hear your aspirations, Master.' The Master said: 'To bring comfort to the old, to be of good faith with friends, and to cherish the young.'

27. The Master said: 'It is all over! I have never come across anyone capable of discerning his errors and inwardly bringing himself to justice.'

28. The Master said: 'In a community of ten households there will certainly be someone as loyal and trustworthy as I am, but not someone so fond of learning as I am.'

1. The Master said: 'Yong may be made to face south.'*
2. When Zhonggong asked about Zisang Bozi, the Master said: 'He is all right, he is easygoing.' Zhonggong said: 'Surely it is all right if one adopts easygoing practices for the sake of dealing with the people provided that one occupies a basic position which commands respect; but if one adopts easygoing practices because one is basically easygoing, surely this is to be too easygoing?' The Master said: 'Yong's words are true.'
3. Duke Ai asked which of the disciples was considered fond of learning. Master Kong replied: 'There was a certain Yan Hui. He was fond of learning. He did not vent his anger on those who did not deserve it, and he did not repeat an error. Unfortunately his allotted span of life was short and he died. As far as the present moment is concerned, he is no longer with us, and I have not yet heard of anyone who is fond of learning.'
4. When Gongxi Hua was sent on a mission to Qi, Master Ran* asked for grain for his mother. The Master said: 'Give her a *fu*.' He asked for more. He said: 'Give her a *yu*.' Master Ran gave her five *bing** of grain. The Master said: 'When Chi went to Qi, he was drawn by well-fed horses and wore light furs. I have heard that the gentleman helps those who are in straitened circumstances and does not maintain the wealthy.'
5. When Yuan Si became steward on the Master's behalf, he was given nine hundred measures of grain, but he declined. 'Do not', said the Master. 'Make use of it for gifts in your local communities.'
6. The Master said of Zhonggong: 'If the offspring of a brindled ox* be red and horned, even if one wished not to use it, would the hills and streams reject it?'
7. The Master said: 'As far as Hui is concerned, his mind for three months does not stray from humaneness; but as for the rest of them, they attain it occasionally, but that is all.'

8. Ji Kang Zi asked whether Zilu was fit to be appointed to join the government. The Master said: 'He is efficient, so what difficulty would there be in his joining the government?' He asked whether Zigong was fit to be appointed to join the government. He said: 'He is perceptive, so what difficulty would there be in his joining the government?' He asked whether Ran You was fit to be appointed to join the government. He said: 'He is accomplished, so what difficulty would there be in his joining the government?'

9. The Ji family appointed Min Ziqian to be steward of Bi.* Min Ziqian said: 'Decline the offer for me skilfully. If there is anyone who comes back for me, I shall certainly be beside the Wen.'*

10. Boniu was ill. The Master enquired after him and, grasping his hand through the window, he said: 'We are losing him. It is fate, isn't it? That such a man should have such a disease, that such a man should have such a disease!'

11. The Master said: 'A man of quality indeed was Hui! He lived in a squalid alley with a tiny bowlful of rice to eat and a ladleful of water to drink. Other men would not endure such hardships, but Hui did not let his happiness be affected. A man of quality indeed was Hui!'

12. Ran You said: 'It is not that I do not feel pleased with your Way, but my strength is inadequate.' The Master said: 'Those whose strength is inadequate fall out along the way, but now you are already imposing limits.'

13. The Master said to Zixia: 'You are to become a gentleman *ru** and avoid being a *ru* who is a small man.'

14. Ziyou became steward of Wucheng. The Master said: 'Have you got anybody there at all?' He said: 'There is a certain Tantai Mieming, who never takes short cuts and except on public business has never once been to my house.'

15. The Master said: 'Meng Zhifan* did not boast. When they fled, he brought up the rear. When they were about to enter the gate, he whipped his horses saying: 'It is not that I have the courage to stay behind. It is just that my horses do not go forward.'

16. The Master said: 'If you do not possess the eloquence of the priest Tuo, it is difficult to get away with things in the

present age even if you possess the beauty of Zhao* of Song.'

17. The Master said: 'Who can go out without using the door? So why is it that nobody follows this Way?'

18. The Master said: 'When substance prevails over refinement there is churlishness, and when refinement prevails over substance there is pedantry. Only if refinement and substance are properly blended, does one become a gentleman.'

19. The Master said: 'The fact that a man lives is due to uprightness. If he spends his life doing without it, he is lucky to survive.'

20. The Master said: 'Those who understand a thing are not equal to those who are fond of it, and those who are fond of it are not equal to those who delight in it.'

21. The Master said: 'Those who are better than average may talk about superior matters, but those who are worse than average may not talk about superior matters.'

22. Fan Chi asked about wisdom. The Master said: 'To work hard at what is right for the people, and to show reverence for ghosts and spirits so as to keep them at a distance* may be called wisdom.' He asked about humaneness. The Master said: 'The humane man puts difficulties first and success in overcoming them second. This may be called humaneness.'

23. The Master said: 'The wise delight in water, but the humane delight in mountains. For although the wise are active, the humane are at rest. And although the wise will find joy, the humane will have long life.'

24. The Master said: 'With one change Qi would come up to Lu, and with one change Lu would reach the Way.'

25. The Master said: 'Even if a *gu** is not used as a *gu*, it is indeed a *gu*, it is indeed a *gu*.'

26. Zai Wo asked: 'Although he be told that there is another humane man in a well, will the humane man join him?' The Master said: 'Why should he do so? The gentleman may be made to go there, but he cannot be submerged in the well. He may be deceived, but he cannot be entrapped.'

27. The Master said: 'The gentleman, with his wide-ranging studies in culture restrained by the requirements of ritual, surely cannot rebel against this, can he?'

28. When the Master went to see Nanzi,* Zilu was displeased. Our Master swore an oath about this, saying: 'What I have failed to do may Heaven reject, may Heaven reject!'

29. The Master said: 'Supreme indeed is the Mean* as a virtue, but for a long time it has been rare among the people.'

30. Zigong said: 'Suppose there were someone who benefited the people far and wide and was capable of bringing salvation to the multitude, what would you think of him? Might he be called humane?' The Master said: 'Why only humane? He would undoubtedly be a sage. Didn't even Yao and Shun* have to take pains over this? Now the humane man, wishing himself to be established, sees that others are established, and wishing himself to be successful, sees that others are successful. To be able to take one's own familiar feelings as a guide may definitely be called the method of humaneness.'

28. When the Master went to see Nanzi, Zilu was displeased. Our Master swore an oath about this, saying: 'What I have failed to do may Heaven reject, may Heaven reject!'
29. The Master said: 'Supreme indeed is the Mean,* as a virtue, but for a long time it has been rare among the people.

BOOK 7

1. The Master said: 'I transmit but do not create. Being fond of the truth, I am an admirer of antiquity. I venture to be compared with our old Peng.'*

2. The Master said: 'I silently accumulate knowledge of things; when I study, I do not get bored; in teaching others I do not grow weary—for these things surely present me with no difficulty.'

3. The Master said: 'The failure to cultivate virtue, the failure to put into practice what I have learnt, hearing what is right and being unable to move towards it, being unable to change what is not good—these are my worries.'

4. When the Master was at leisure, he was relaxed and comfortable.

5. The Master said: 'Extreme is my decline; it is long since I last dreamt I saw the Duke of Zhou!'*

6. The Master said: 'Set your heart on the Way, base yourself on virtue, rely on humaneness, and take your relaxation in the arts.'

7. The Master said: 'From the bringer of a bundle of dried meat* upwards, I have never once refused instruction to anyone.'

8. The Master said: 'To those who are not eager to learn I do not explain anything, and to those who are not bursting to speak I do not reveal anything. If I raise one angle and they do not come back with the other three angles, I will not repeat myself.'

9. When the Master was eating alongside someone in mourning, he never ate his fill.

10. If on a certain day he had wept the Master did not sing.

11. The Master said to Yan Hui: 'To take action wnen employed and to remain in store* when dismissed—surely only you and I have this capacity.' Zilu said: 'If you, Master, were leading the three armies,* then who would go with you?' The Master said: 'I would not go with anyone who

had no regrets if he died tackling a tiger with his bare hands or crossing the Yellow River without a boat. What would be necessary would be someone who was apprehensive when approaching a task and liked achieving success through planning.'

12. The Master said: 'If even riches might properly be sought, I would surely make them my aim, even if it meant being a fellow carrying a whip;* but if they may not be properly sought, I shall pursue those things which I admire.'

13. What the Master took trouble over were fasting, war, and sickness.

14. When the Master was in Qi, he heard the *shao*, and for three months did not notice the taste of meat. He said: 'I did not imagine that music-making reached such perfection.'

15. Ran You said: 'Is our Master in favour of the Lord of Wei?'* Zigong said: 'All right, I shall ask about that.' He went in and said: 'What sort of men were Bo Yi and Shu Qi?' He said: 'They were men of quality from ancient times.' He said: 'Did they feel resentment?' He said: 'They sought humaneness and obtained humaneness, so what would they resent?' When he came out he said: 'Our Master is not in favour.'

16. The Master said: 'Even in the midst of eating coarse rice and drinking water and using a bent arm for a pillow happiness is surely to be found; riches and honours acquired by unrighteous means are to me like the floating clouds.'

17. The Master said: 'Give me a few more years so that I am studying at fifty, and surely I may avoid major errors.'

18. What the Master used the standard pronunciation* for were the *Songs*, the *Documents*, and the performance of the rites. For all these he used the standard pronunciation.

19. The Duke of She asked Zilu about Master Kong. Zilu did not reply. The Master said: 'Why did you not just say that he is the sort of person who gets so worked up that he forgets to eat, is so happy that he forgets anxieties, and is not aware that old age will come.'

20. The Master said: 'I am not one who knew about things at birth; I am one who through my admiration of antiquity is keen to discover things.'

21. The Master did not speak of* prodigies, force, disorders, or spirits.

22. The Master said: 'When I walk with two others, I always receive instruction from them. I select their good qualities and copy them, and improve on their bad qualities.'

23. The Master said: 'Heaven produced virtue in me, so what will Huan Tui* have to do with me?'

24. The Master said: 'My friends, do you consider me secretive? I definitely have no secrets. I am one who shares with you, my friends, every step he takes. Such a one am I.'

25. The Master took four subjects for his teaching: culture, conduct, loyalty, and good faith.

26. The Master said: 'A sage I have not been able to meet, but a person who manages to meet a gentleman will do.' The Master said: 'A good man I have not been able to meet, but a person who manages to meet a man of constancy will do. But when people pretend to possess things they do not have, pretend to be full when they are empty, pretend to be prosperous when they are in straitened circumstances, it is indeed difficult to maintain constancy.'

27. The Master used a line, but did not trawl for fish; he used a corded arrow,* but did not shoot at sitting targets.

28. The Master said: 'Surely there are people who achieve something without knowledge, but I for my part lack this characteristic. To hear much and select the good points from it and copy them, to see much and remember it constitutes an inferior variety of knowledge.'*

29. In Hu village it was difficult to hold conversations with the people; so when a lad presented himself, the disciples had their doubts. The Master said: 'I shall be associating with his coming into my presence, not with what he does after he has withdrawn from it. Just what are you being so serious about? If a man purifies himself* in order to be admitted into my presence, I am associating with the fact that he has been purified, and I am not vouching for his past.'

30. The Master said: 'Is humaneness really so far away? If we ourselves wanted humaneness, then humaneness would arrive.'

31. The Minister of Crime of Chen asked whether Duke

Zhao understood the rites. Master Kong said: 'He understood the rites.' When Master Kong withdrew, he bowed to Wuma Qi and made him come forward. He said: 'I have heard that gentlemen do not have favourites, but surely the gentleman does? The ruler took to wife a lady of Wu with the same surname as himself, but called her Wu Meng Zi.* If even he understood the rites, who does not understand the rites?' Wuma Qi reported this. The Master said: 'I am fortunate. If I have faults, other people are certain to be aware of them.'

32. When the Master was singing with others, he always had the good bits repeated before joining in.

33. The Master said: 'In making an effort I am comparable with others, but as to myself being a gentleman in practice, I have never yet managed to achieve that.'

34. The Master said: 'As for being a sage or a humane man, I would surely not presume to be such? On the other hand it may simply be said that I do not get tired of aiming for this and do not grow weary of teaching others.' Gongxi Hua said: 'It is just that we disciples are incapable of following your example.'

35. The Master was gravely ill and Zilu requested to say a prayer. The Master said: 'Does such a thing happen?' Zilu replied: 'Yes, it does. The prayer for the dead says: "We pray thus to the spirits above and below."' The Master said: 'My prayers have been going on for a long time.'*

36. The Master said: 'If one is extravagant, then one becomes imprudent; if one is frugal, then one becomes inflexible. It is better for one to be set in one's ways than imprudent.'

37. The Master said: 'The gentleman is calm and peaceful; the small man is always emotional.'

38. The Master was genial and yet strict, imposing and yet not intimidating, courteous and yet at ease.

BOOK 8

1. The Master said: 'Surely Tai Bo* may be said to have reached the extremes of virtue. Three times he renounced the right to rule over all under Heaven, but the people had no chance to offer him praise.'

2. The Master said: 'If one is courteous but does without ritual, then one dissipates one's energies; if one is cautious but does without ritual, then one becomes timid; if one is bold but does without ritual, then one becomes reckless; if one is forthright but does without ritual, then one becomes rude. When gentlemen deal sincerely with their kinsfolk, then the people are stimulated towards humaneness. When old friends are not neglected, then the people will not behave irresponsibly.'

3. When Master Zeng was ill, he summoned the disciples of his school and said: 'Uncover my feet, uncover my hands. The *Song* says:

> In fear and trembling
> As though approaching a deep abyss,
> As though treading on thin ice.

But for now and hereafter I know that I have come through safely,* haven't I, my young friends?'

4. When Master Zeng was ill, Meng Jing Zi asked after him. Master Zeng said: 'When a bird is about to die, its song is mournful; but when a man is about to die, his words are good. The things which the gentleman values in the Way are three: in transforming his demeanour he banishes violence and rudeness, in composing his expression he keeps close to sincerity, and in the style of his utterances he banishes coarseness and impropriety. As to the business of sacrificial vessels, the officials will attend to that.'

5. Master Zeng said: 'Although he was able, he put questions to those who were not; although he had many talents, he put questions to those who had few; he had yet he

appeared to lack, he was full yet he seemed empty; although
he was offended against, he did not fight back. At one time
my friend* always used to devote his efforts to these ends.'
6. Master Zeng said: 'If one could entrust a man with the
care of a young orphan and could also commission him with
the command over a territory of a hundred *li* square and he
could not be deflected when facing a crisis, would he be a
gentleman? He would be a gentleman.'
7. Master Zeng said: 'The public servant must be broad-
shouldered and stout-hearted. His burden is heavy and his
way is long. For humaneness is the burden he has taken on
himself; is it not true that it is a heavy one to bear? Only
with death does his journey end; is it not true that he has far
to go?'
8. The Master said: 'One is roused by the *Songs*, established by ritual, and perfected by music.'
9. The Master said: 'The people may be made to follow
something, but may not be made to understand it.'
10. The Master said: 'Love of courage and hatred of
poverty brings lawlessness. Excessive hatred of those who are
not humane although human also results in lawlessness.'
11. The Master said: 'Even if one had talents as attractive
as the Duke of Zhou, supposing one were also arrogant and
mean, the rest of one's qualities would simply not be worthy
of notice.'
12. The Master said: 'It is not easy to find anyone who
studies for three years but is not intent on* a salary.'
13. The Master said: 'Be of sincere good faith and love
learning. Be steadfast unto death in pursuit of the good Way.
One does not enter a state which is in peril, nor reside in one
which is rebellious. When the Way prevails in the world,
then be seen. When it does not, then hide. When the Way
prevails in your own state, to be made poor and obscure
by it is a disgrace; but when the Way does not prevail in
your own state, to be made rich and honourable by it is a
disgrace.'
14. The Master said: 'If one is not in a certain office, one
does not plan the governance involved in that office.'
15. The Master said: 'When the music-master Zhi starts to

play and when the climax of the *Guan ju* is reached, what a flood of sound fills one's ears!'

16. The Master said: 'Headstrong and yet not straightforward, simple-minded and yet not sincere, guileless and yet not true to their word—I do not understand such people.'

17. The Master said: 'Even if one studies as if it will not be attained, one is still afraid of failing to reach it.'

18. The Master said: 'How sublime was the way in which Shun and Yu* possessed all under Heaven but remained aloof from it!'

19. The Master said: 'Great indeed was Yao as a ruler! Sublime indeed was he! It is only Heaven that may be deemed great, but only Yao modelled himself upon it. So boundless was he that the people were without the ability to put a name to him. Sublime was he in the works which he achieved and glorious in the accomplishments which he possessed.'

20. Shun had five ministers and all under Heaven was well governed, and King Wu said: 'I have ten ministers who are skilled in government.' Master Kong commented: 'Is it not true that talent is hard to find? At the time of Shun's accession things are thought to have flourished, and with a woman among King Wu's ministers, there were in fact only nine men. Yet he held two-thirds of all under Heaven and with this served the Yin. The virtue of Zhou* may indeed be called perfect virtue.'

21. The Master said: 'In Yu it seems there is no fault as far as I am concerned. Although he ate and drank abstemiously, he displayed the utmost devotion* towards the ghosts and spirits. Although normally he wore poor garments, he displayed the utmost elegance in his sacrificial robes and headdress. He lived in humble dwellings, but devoted all his energies to drains and ditches. In Yu it seems there is no fault as far as I am concerned.'

BOOK 9

1.* The Master seldom spoke of profit and fate and humaneness.

2. A villager from Daxiang said: 'Great indeed is Master Kong, but despite his broad learning there is nothing for which he has made a reputation.' When the Master heard this, he told his disciples: 'What do I take up? Do I take up charioteering?* Or do I take up archery? I take up charioteering.'

3. The Master said: 'A linen cap is prescribed by the rites, but nowadays people use black silk. This is thrifty and I follow the multitude. To do obeisance below is prescribed by the rites, but nowadays people do obeisance after ascending.* This is arrogant and, although I go against the multitude, I follow the rule of doing so below.'

4. The Master cut out four things. He never took anything for granted, he never insisted on certainty, he was never inflexible and never egotistical.

5. When the Master was intimidated at Kuang,* he said: 'When King Wen died, was culture not still here? If Heaven had intended to put an end to this culture, later mortals would not have been able to share in it. If Heaven is not yet putting an end to this culture, what have the people of Kuang got to do with me?'

6. The Grand Steward asked Zigong: 'Your Master is a sage, is he not? For what about his many abilities?' Zigong said: 'Certainly Heaven granted that he would become a sage, but he also has many abilities.' When the Master heard this, he said: 'Does the Grand Steward understand me? When I was young, I was in humble circumstances, and therefore I acquired many abilities in menial matters. Does the gentleman really have many abilities? No, not many.'

7. Lao says that the Master said: 'It is because I have not yet been tried out in office that I have developed accomplishments.'

8. The Master said: 'Do I for my part really possess under-

standing? No, I do not possess understanding. But if there is an ordinary person putting a question to me, although his mind seems to be quite blank, I hammer at both sides of the question and go into it thoroughly.'

9. The Master said: 'The phoenix does not come and the river does not give forth a chart.* I am finished, aren't I?'

10. When the Master encountered people wearing mourning dress or ceremonial headdress and robes or people who were blind, even if they were younger than himself, he always rose to his feet when he saw them and, when he passed them, he always made haste.*

11. Yan Hui, sighing heavily, said: 'The more I look up to it,* the higher it is; the more I penetrate it, the harder it becomes; I see it ahead of me and suddenly it is behind. Our Master skilfully lures people on step by step. He broadens me with culture and restrains me with ritual. If I wanted to stop, I could not; and when I have exhausted all my talents, it seems as if there is something which he has established profoundly; but even though I long to pursue it, I have no way of doing so at all.'

12. When the Master was gravely ill, Zilu made the disciples act as his official underlings.* During a remission in the illness he said: 'For a long time indeed has You's behaviour been deceitful. In being deemed to have official underlings when I have none, whom do I deceive? Do I deceive Heaven? Moreover would it not be preferable for me to die in your hands, my friends, rather than that I should be in the hands of official underlings? And besides, granted that I shall not get a big funeral, am I dying at the wayside?'

13. Zigong said: 'Suppose there is a beautiful jade* here, does one wrap it up, put it in a box and keep it, or does one try to get a good price and sell it?' The Master said: 'Sell it of course, sell it of course! I am one who is waiting for a price.'

14. The Master wished to dwell among the nine wild tribes of the East. Someone said: 'They are uncivilized, so what will you do about that?' The Master said: 'If a gentleman dwelt among them, what lack of civility would they show?'

15. The Master said: 'It was only after I had returned from

Wei to Lu that music was rectified, with the *ya* and the *song**
each getting their places.'

16. The Master said: 'Serving the ruler and high ministers
outside the family and parents and elders inside the family,
not daring not to put every effort into matters of mourning,
and not being the worse for wine—surely these present me
with no difficulties.'

17. When the Master was standing by a stream, he said:
'Things that go past are like this, aren't they? For they do not
set aside day or night.'

18. The Master said: 'I have never come across anyone
who admires virtue as much as he admires sexual attraction.'

19. The Master said: 'Just as when making a mound, if I
stop when only one basketful is needed to complete it, it will
be my own stopping; and just as when levelling the earth,
even if I have tipped out only one basketful, the progress
made is my own advance.'

20. The Master said: 'The one who does not flag when I
am speaking to him is surely Hui, isn't it?'

21. The Master said of Yan Hui: 'Alas! I saw that he was
making progress, but I never saw that he was stopping.'*

22. The Master said: 'There are times, aren't there, when
plants shoot but do not flower, and when they flower but do
not produce fruit?'

23. The Master said: 'The young should be revered, for
how does one know that what is to come will not be as good
as the present? If they were forty or fifty and nothing had
been learnt from them, then presumably they would not be
worthy of reverence at all.'

24. The Master said: 'Can one avoid concurring with
exemplary sayings? But to make them the basis of self-
improvement is considered the most valuable thing. Can one
avoid being pleased with blandishments? But to unravel the
motivation is considered the most valuable thing. If someone
is pleased but does not unravel the motivation, concurs but
does not improve himself, I can do nothing for him at all.'

25. The Master said: 'Regard loyalty and good faith as
your main concern. Do not make friends of those who are

not up to your own standard. If you commit a fault, do not shrink from correcting it.'

26. The Master said: 'The three armies can be robbed of their commander, but an ordinary person cannot be robbed of his purpose.'

27. The Master said: 'It will be You, won't it, who is the one who wears a shabby robe padded with silk floss and does not feel ashamed at standing side by side with someone wearing fox or badger.

> Neither wicked nor greedy,
> Why is he not good?'

Zilu was always chanting these lines,* but the Master said: 'How is such a Way adequate for the achievement of goodness.'

28. The Master said: 'It is only when the year turns cold that one becomes aware that pine and cypress are the last to fade.'

29. The Master said: 'The wise are not perplexed, the humane do not worry, and the courageous do not feel fear.'

30. The Master said: 'It is possible to study together with someone although it is not possible to pursue the Way with him; it is possible to pursue the Way with someone although it is not possible to take a stand with him; it is possible to take a stand with someone although it is not possible to weigh things up with him.'

31.*

> The flowers of the wild cherry
> Blow hither and thither.
> Truly I think of you,
> But your house is far away.

The Master said: 'He never thought of her, for there really is no such thing as being far away.'

pleasant expression. At private audiences he seemed at ease.
5. The gentleman does not use violet or mauve adornments, and does not use red or purple in his informal dress. During hot weather he wears an unlined garment of fine or

BOOK 10*

1. In the local community Master Kong was rather unassuming and seemed as if he were an inarticulate person; but in the ancestral temple or at court he spoke readily but cautiously. At court, when speaking with lower grandees he was affable, and when speaking with higher grandees he was forthright. When the ruler was present he was respectful but self-possessed.

2. When the ruler summoned him to receive a guest, his expression became serious and his step brisk. When he bowed to those with whom he was standing, his hands reached out to left and right and his robes seemed to shake as he went back and forth, and yet as he hastened forward, he seemed to glide as if on wings. When the guest had departed, he always reported: 'The guest does not look back.'

3. When he entered the palace gate, he seemed to gather himself in as if it would not admit him. When he stood still, he did not occupy the centre of the gateway, and when he moved forward, he did not step on the threshold. When he passed the ruler's position, his expression became serious and his step brisk, and his words seemed inadequate. When he ascended the hall, holding up the hem of his garment, he seemed to gather himself in, and he held his breath and seemed like someone who was not breathing. When he came out, having descended one step, he wore a more relaxed expression and seemed relieved. When he reached the bottom of the steps, he hastened forward and seemed to glide as if on wings, and when he returned to his position he looked respectful.

4. When he held the jade tablet, he gathered himself in as if he could not cope with it. At the highest he held it as if he were bowing, and at the lowest as if he were making a presentation. His expression became serious and apprehensive, and his feet were constricted as if his progress were hindered. When he presented ritual gifts, he wore a com-

plaisant expression. At private audiences he seemed at ease.

5. The gentleman does not use purple or mauve adornments, and does not use red or vermilion for informal dress. During hot weather he wears an unlined garment of fine or coarse material, but he always wears it on the outside to show it off. With a black robe he wears lambskin, with an undyed robe he wears fawnskin, and with a yellow robe he wears fox fur. His informal fur coat is long, but it has a short right sleeve. He always has sleeping clothes which are half as long again as his whole body. Thick furs of fox or badger are used for staying at home. When he leaves off mourning, he wears all his girdle-ornaments. Except for ceremonial skirts he always has things cut out. Lambskin garments and black caps are not used for visits of condolence. On the first day of the month he always puts on court dress and goes to court. When he is purifying himself, he always wears a spirit robe made of cotton.

6. When he is purifying himself, he always changes his diet, and also, when he is at home, he shifts the place where he sits. When he eats, he is not sated with fine rice, nor with finely minced meat. Rice which has turned sour and fish and meat which has gone off he does not eat. When the colour or smell of the food has gone bad, he does not eat. What has not been properly cooked he does not eat. He does not eat except at the proper time. If the food is not properly cut up, he does not eat; and if he cannot get the sauce for it, he does not eat. Even if the meat is plentiful, he does not let it be more abundant than the rice. Only wine has no limit, but he does not go so far as to be fuddled. Wine or dried meat bought in the shops he does not eat. Although he does not have food with ginger in it cleared away, he does not eat much. When sacrifices have been made by the duke, he does not keep the sacrificial meat overnight; and indeed sacrificial meat in general is not kept beyond three days. After three days have been exceeded, he does not eat it. When eating he does not converse, nor does he talk in bed. Even when sacrificing coarse rice or vegetable broth, he always does so with reverence.

7. If the mat were not straight, he did not sit. When the

villagers were having a drink of wine, he left when those who carried walking-sticks had left.

8.   When the villagers were exorcizing evil spirits, he put on his court robes and stood on the eastern steps.*

9.   When enquiring about someone in another state, he saw the messenger off with two obeisances.

10.   When Ji Kang Zi sent him some medicine, he made obeisance and accepted it, but said: 'I do not understand it at all so I do not dare taste it.'

11.   When the stables caught fire the Master, on returning from court, said: 'Did anyone get hurt?' He did not ask about the horses.

12.   When the ruler bestowed food upon him, he always adjusted his mat and then was the first to taste it. When the ruler bestowed uncooked food upon him, he always offered it up after it had been cooked. If the ruler bestowed on him something still alive, he always reared it. When he was in attendance at a feast given by the ruler, the ruler sacrificed and then started on the rice.

13.   When the ruler came to see him when he was ill, although he had his head to the east,* he had his court clothing put on top of him with the sash hanging down.

14.   When he was summoned by the ruler's command, he set off, not waiting for horses to be yoked to his carriage.

15.   When he entered the grand temple, he asked questions about every single thing.

16.   When a friend died, if there was nowhere to restore him to, he said: 'It is up to me to organize the funeral.' Before a gift from a friend, even if it were a carriage or horses, he did not make obeisance as he would have done if it had been sacrificial meat.

17.   When in bed he did not adopt the posture of a corpse. When at home he did not adopt the attitude of a guest.

18.   When he met anyone wearing mourning garb, even if he was on familiar terms with him, he always changed countenance. If he met someone wearing a ceremonial cap or a blind person, even if he was in informal attire, he always adopted the appropriate demeanour. Anyone wearing mourning attire he would bow to, touching the front bar of

his carriage, and he would do the same to anyone carrying tablets. Whenever sumptuous delicacies appeared, he always changed countenance and stood up. When there was a sudden clap of thunder or the wind turned violent, he always changed countenance.

19.   When he climbed into a carriage, he always stood straight and grasped the mounting-cord. Inside the carriage he did not face inwards, did not speak hastily, and did not point.

20.*   It rises up at the appearance, hovers about and then settles.

21.   He said: 'How timely is the pheasant on the mountain bridge!' Zilu showed his reverence for it, but it flapped its wings three times and rose.

BOOK 11

1. The Master said: 'Those who first approached me were rustics as far as rites and music were concerned, and those who approached me afterwards were gentlemen as far as rites and music were concerned. If I put them to use, I follow those who first approached me.'

2. The Master said: 'All of those who accompanied me in Chen and Cai do not reach my door.'

3. Virtuous conduct:* Yan Hui, Min Ziqian, Ran Boniu and Zhonggong; speech: Zai Wo and Zigong; administration: Ran You and Zilu; culture and learning: Ziyou and Zixia.

4. The Master said: 'Hui is not a person who helps me. In my words there is nothing which he does not admire.'

5. The Master said: 'Filial indeed is Min Ziqian, for other people do not find any flaw in his parents' and brothers' reports.'

6. Nan Rong frequently repeated the piece about the white jade sceptre,* so Master Kong gave him his elder brother's daughter in marriage.

7. Ji Kang Zi asked which of the disciples was considered fond of learning. Master Kong replied: 'There was a certain Yan Hui. He was fond of learning, but unfortunately his allotted span was short and he died. As far as the present is concerned, there is no one.'

8. When Yan Hui died, Yan Lu* asked for the Master's carriage so as to provide him with an outer coffin. The Master said: 'Talented or untalented, to be sure each person talks about his own son. When Li died, he had an inner but not an outer coffin. I would not go on foot in order to provide him with an outer coffin, for since I follow after the grandees, it is not proper for me to go on foot.'

9. When Yan Hui died, the Master said: 'Alas, Heaven has bereaved me, Heaven has bereaved me!'

10. When Yan Hui died, the Master became distressed as he bewailed him. His followers said: 'Master, you have

become distressed.' 'Have I?' he said. 'Well, if that man is not to be the object of my distress, then for whom am I to be distressed?'

11. When Yan Hui died, the disciples wanted to give him a lavish funeral. The Master said that it would be improper, but the disciples gave him a lavish funeral. The Master said: 'Hui looked upon me as a father, but I have not been able to look upon him as a son. But it is not because of me, it is because of these gentlemen.'

12. Zilu asked about serving ghosts and spirits. The Master said: 'If one is not yet capable of serving men,* how can one serve ghosts?' He ventured to ask about the dead, and the Master said: 'If one does not yet understand life, how does one understand death?'

13. When they stood at his side in attendance on him, Min Ziqian looked upright, Zilu looked resolute, Ran You and Zigong looked courteous. The Master was happy.

  A man like You* will not attain his span of years.

14. When the men of Lu were working on the Long Treasury, Min Ziqian said: 'Why not restore it? Why must it be rebuilt?' The Master said: 'That man does not normally have anything to say, but when he does he is always on target.'

15. The Master said: 'Why is You's zithern* at my door?' so the disciples ceased to respect Zilu. The Master therefore said: 'You has ascended to the reception-hall, although he has not yet entered the inner apartments.'

16. Zigong asked which was of the higher quality, Zizhang or Zixia. The Master said: 'Shi goes beyond and Shang does not arrive.' 'If this is so', he said, 'then Shi is the superior, is he not?' The Master said: 'To go beyond is no different from not arriving.'

17. The Ji family was wealthier than the Duke of Zhou, and yet Ran You increased their wealth by collecting revenues on their behalf. The Master said: 'He is not a disciple of mine. It is all right for you, my friends, to sound the drum* and attack him.'

18. Chai* is moronic, Can is slow-witted, Shi is disdainful, and You is crude.

The Master said: 'Hui is perhaps near the mark but he is often hard up. Si does not accept his lot, so his goods and chattels have become abundant through this. But when he does indulge in reflection, he is often on target.

19.   Zizhang enquired about the way of the good man. The Master said: 'He does not tread in others' footsteps, and therefore does not enter the inner apartments.'

The Master said: 'He sides with sincerity in discussion, but is he a gentleman, or is he merely grave in his outward appearance?'

20.   Zilu asked whether, if one hears something, one practises it. The Master said: 'Since your father and elder brothers are still alive, how would you, if you heard something, put it into practice?' Ran You asked the same question and the Master said that when one hears something one practises it. Gongxi Hua said: 'Zilu asked whether, if one hears something, one practises it; and you, Master, said that his father and elder brothers were still alive; but when Ran You asked the same question, you, Master, said that when one hears something one should practise it. I am perplexed and venture to question this.' The Master said: 'Qiu is backward and so I urged him on, but You is an over-enthusiastic person and so I held him back.'

21.   When the Master was intimidated at Kuang, Yan Hui fell behind. The Master said: 'I thought you were dead.' He said: 'While you are alive, Master, how shall I presume to die?'

22.   Ji Ziran asked whether Zilu and Ran You could be called great ministers. The Master said: 'I thought it was unusual people you were asking about, but instead it is only You and Qiu you ask about. What I call a great minister serves his ruler in accordance with the Way, and when it is impossible to do so he resigns. Now You and Qiu may be described as ministers appointed to make up the number.' He said: 'If this is so then are they the sort of people who are always obedient?' The Master said: 'If it comes to assassinating their father or ruler, they would surely not obey.'

23.   Zilu had Zigao* made steward of Bi. The Master said:

'He is injuring another man's son.' Zilu said: 'There are the people there and there are the altars of the land and grain there. Why must one read books before one can be considered to have learnt?' The Master said: 'This is why I hate those who have persuasive tongues.'

24.   Zilu, Zeng Xi,* Ran You, and Gongxi Hua were seated in attendance when the Master said: 'Although I am a little bit older than you, don't take it into account. Since you are out of office, you say that you are not appreciated. But if someone were to appreciate you, how would you in fact behave?' Zilu promptly replied: 'If there were a state of a thousand chariots, precariously situated between major states which attacked it with their armies so that it suffered famine, and if I were to run it, then before three years were up its people could be made to have courage and furthermore to know which way they were going.' Our Master smiled at him. 'Qiu, what about you?' He replied: 'If there were a state of sixty to seventy or maybe fifty to sixty *li* square and I were to run it, then before three years were up it could be made to have a sufficient population; but as for its rites and music, they would await a gentleman.' 'And Chi, what about you?' He replied: 'It is not that I would say I am capable of these things, but I would like to devote study to them. At the ceremonies in the ancestral temple or at diplomatic gatherings I should like to play the part of a junior assistant there, dressed in the appropriate cap and robes.' 'Dian, what about you?' He was playing the zithern and, when the sound of the instrument stopped, he put it aside and got up and replied: 'It is different from the choice of these three gentlemen.' The Master said: 'What harm is there? Surely each man states his own ambitions.' He said: 'In late spring, when the spring robes have been made, with five or six capped youths and six or seven uncapped boys, I would bathe in the Yi, feel the breeze at the dancing sacrifice* and return home chanting.' Our Master heaved a deep sigh and said: 'I am on the side of Dian.' When the other three left Zeng Xi stayed behind. 'What about the remarks of these three gentlemen?' he said. The Master said: 'Surely each man was stating his own ambitions and that's all.' He said: 'Why did our Master smile

at You?' He said: 'If one runs a state, one makes use of the rites. In his remarks he showed no deference, and so I smiled at him.' 'In the case of Qiu it was not a state, was it?' 'Where have you seen a domain of sixty to seventy or even fifty to sixty *li* square which was not a state?' 'In the case of Chi it was not a state, was it?' 'As for ancestral temples and diplomatic gatherings, who are they for if not for the rulers of states? And if Chi were playing a small part in such matters, who could take a major role?'

BOOK 12

1. Yan Hui asked about humaneness. The Master said: 'To subdue oneself and return to ritual is to practise humaneness. If someone subdued himself and returned to ritual for a single day, then all under Heaven would ascribe humaneness to him. For the practice of humaneness does surely proceed from the man himself, or does it proceed from others?' Yan Hui said: 'I beg to ask for the details of this.' The Master said: 'Do not look at what is contrary to ritual, do not listen to what is contrary to ritual, do not speak what is contrary to ritual, and make no movement which is contrary to ritual.' Yan Hui said: 'Although I am not clever, I beg to put this advice into practice.'

2. Zhonggong asked about humaneness. The Master said: 'When you are away from home, behave as if receiving an important guest. Employ the people as if you were officiating at a great sacrifice. Do not impose on others what you would not like yourself. Then there will be no resentment against you, either in the state or in the family.' Zhonggong said: 'Although I am not clever, I beg to put this advice into practice.'

3. Sima Niu asked about humaneness. The Master said: 'The humane person is hesitant in his speech.' He said: 'Hesitant in his speech! Is that all that is meant by humaneness?' The Master said: 'To do it is difficult, so in speaking about it can one avoid being hesitant?'

4. Sima Niu asked about the gentleman. The Master said: 'The gentleman is neither worried nor afraid.' He said: 'Neither worried nor afraid! Is that all that is meant by the gentleman?' The Master said: 'If when he looks within he is not diseased, then what does he worry about and what does he fear?'

5. 'Other men all have brothers', said Sima Niu* in his distress, 'but I alone have none.' Zixia said: 'I have heard that death and life are predestined, and riches and honours depend on Heaven. If a gentleman is reverent and avoids

error, if he is courteous in his dealings with others and observes the obligations of ritual, then all within the Four Seas are his brothers. Why should a gentleman be distressed at not having brothers?'

6. Zizhang asked about intelligence. The Master said: 'If slanders which gradually seep in or accusations like flesh-wounds do not get anywhere with one, one may definitely be called intelligent. But if slanders which gradually seep in or accusations like flesh-wounds do not get anywhere with one, one may definitely also be called distant.'

7. Zigong asked about government. The Master said: 'If there is enough food and if there are enough weapons, the people will put their trust in it.' Zigong said: 'Suppose you definitely had no alternative but to give up one of these three, which would you relinquish first?' The Master said: 'I would give up weapons.' Zigong said: 'Suppose you definitely had no alternative but to give up one of the remaining two, which would you relinquish first?' The Master said: 'I would give up food. From of old death has come to all men, but a people will not stand if it lacks trust.'*

8. Ji Zicheng said: 'A gentleman is merely the stuff he is made of. Why take account of culture?' Zigong said: 'It is a pity you said that, sir, about the gentleman, since a team of four horses will not catch up with the tongue. Culture is just as important as the stuff one is made of, and the stuff one is made of is just as important as culture. The skin of a tiger or leopard is no different from the skin of a dog or a sheep.'

9. Duke Ai enquired of Master You: 'The year has seen famine and the revenues are inadequate, so what should be done in such circumstances?' Master You replied: 'Why not take one-tenth of their produce in tax?' He said: 'With two-tenths I would still not have enough, so in that case what would a one-tenth tax achieve?' The reply was: 'If the hundred surnames have plenty, then with whom will your lordship share insufficiency; but if the hundred surnames do not have plenty, with whom will you share plenty?'

10. Zizhang asked about exalting virtue and clearing up confusions. The Master said: 'Exalting virtue consists of making loyalty and good faith into one's main principles and

moving towards rightness. If you love someone you want him to live, but if you hate someone you want him to die. If having wanted him to live you also want him to die, this is confusion.

Not for the sake of riches
But merely for a change.'*

11. Duke Jing of Qi asked Master Kong about government. Master Kong replied: 'Let a ruler be a ruler,* a subject a subject, a father a father, and a son a son.' 'Excellent!' said the Duke. 'Indeed, if a ruler be not a ruler, a subject be not a subject, a father be not a father, and a son be not a son, even if there is grain, shall I manage to eat it?'

12. The Master said: 'The one who might settle a law-suit on the basis of a partial submission would be You, wouldn't it?' Zilu avoided sleeping on a promise.*

13. The Master said: 'At hearing legal proceedings I am no different from anybody else, but what is surely necessary is to bring it about that there is no litigation.'

14. Zizhang asked about government. The Master said: 'When dwelling on a matter, avoid becoming bored; and when taking action on it, observe the requirements of loyalty.'

15. The Master said: 'If wide-ranging studies in culture are restrained by the requirements of ritual, surely one cannot rebel against this, can one?'

16. The Master said: 'The gentleman brings to completion the fine qualities in others and does not bring to completion the bad qualities in others. The small man does the opposite of this.'

17. Ji Kang Zi asked Master Kong about government. Master Kong replied: 'To govern means to correct.* If you take the lead by being correct, who will dare not to be corrected?'

18. Ji Kang Zi was worried about thieves, so he put a question to Master Kong. Master Kong replied: 'If you yourself did not desire these things, they would not steal them even if they were rewarded.'

19. Ji Kang Zi asked Master Kong about government,

saying: 'Suppose I were to kill those who lack the Way in order to advance those who have the Way, how would that be?' Master Kong replied: 'You are running the government, so what is the point of killing? If you desire good, the people will be good. The nature of the gentleman is as the wind, and the nature of the small man* is as the grass. When the wind blows over the grass it always bends.'

20.   Zizhang asked what a public servant would be like so that he might be called successful. The Master said: 'What ever is it that you mean by successful?' Zizhang replied: 'Certain to be heard about, whether employed in the state or in a noble family.' The Master said: 'This is reputation, not success. Now the successful man is by nature straightforward and fond of what is right. He examines what people say and notices their looks and is anxious to give priority to others. He is bound to be successful whether employed in the state or in a noble family. But the man of reputation assumes an air of humaneness although his conduct belies it, and he does not feel any misgivings about persisting in this. Whether employed in the state or in a noble family he will certainly achieve reputation.'

21.   Fan Chi was in attendance at an outing below where the dancing sacrifice took place. He said: 'I venture to ask about exalting virtue, reforming wickedness, and clearing up confusions.' The Master said: 'An excellent question indeed! Putting the job first and what you get out of it last—is this not exalting virtue? Attacking one's own bad qualities and avoiding attacks on other people's bad qualities—is not this the way to reform wickedness? To be oblivious of one's own person and even of one's own parents all because of a morning's anger—is this not a confusion?'

22.   Fan Chi asked about humaneness. The Master said: 'It is to love others.' He asked about understanding. The Master said: 'It is to understand others.' Fan Chi had not yet fathomed his meaning, so the Master said: 'If one raises the straight and puts them above the crooked one can make the crooked become straight.' When Fan Chi withdrew, he met Zixia. 'I was granted an interview by the Master just now', he said, 'and I asked him about understanding. The Master

said: "If one raises the straight and puts them above the crooked one can make the crooked become straight." What did he mean?' 'A rich saying indeed!' said Zixia. 'When Shun possessed all under Heaven, he made a choice from among the multitude and raised up Gao Yao,* and the inhumane were banished; and when Tang possessed all under Heaven, he made a choice from among the multitude and raised up Yi Yin and the inhumane were banished.'

23.   Zigong asked about friends. The Master said: 'Loyally provide them with information and guide them skilfully. If this is no good, then desist. Do not humiliate yourself through them.'

24.   Master Zeng said: 'The gentleman collects friends through culture, and through his friends supports humaneness.'

BOOK 13

1. Zilu asked about government. The Master said: 'By giving them a lead, cause them to work hard.' When he asked for something more, he said 'without getting bored'.

2. Zhonggong, being steward to the Ji family, asked about government. The Master said: 'Give a lead to your officials, pardon minor errors, and promote men of quality and talent.' He said: 'How does one recognize men of quality and talent so as to promote them?' He said: 'Promote those you do recognize, for will others neglect those you do not recognize?'

3. Zilu said: 'If the Lord of Wei were waiting for you to run the government, what would you give priority to?' The Master said: 'What is necessary is to rectify names, is it not?'* Zilu said: 'If this were to take place, it would surely be an aberration of yours. Why should they be rectified?' The Master said: 'How uncivilized you are. With regard to what he does not understand the gentleman is surely somewhat reluctant to offer an opinion. If names are not rectified, then words are not appropriate. If words are not appropriate, then deeds are not accomplished. If deeds are not accomplished, then the rites and music do not flourish. If the rites and music do not flourish, then punishments do not hit the mark. If punishments do not hit the mark, then the people have nowhere to put hand or foot. So when a gentleman names something, the name can definitely be used in speech; and when he says something, it can definitely be put into practice. In his utterances the gentleman is definitely not casual about anything.'

4. Fan Chi asked to be taught how to grow crops. The Master said: 'I am not as good as an old farmer.' He asked to be taught how to manage a vegetable plot. He said: 'I am not as good as an old vegetable-grower.' When Fan Chi left the Master said: 'A small man indeed is Fan Chi. If their superior is fond of ritual, then none of the people will dare not to behave with reverence; if their superior is fond of

what is right, then none of the people will dare not to be obedient; if their superior is fond of good faith, then none of the people will dare not to go by the true circumstances. Now if he is like this, the people on all sides will come to him* with their children strapped on their backs. What is the point of growing crops?'

5. The Master said: 'A man may know by heart the three hundred *Songs*, but if he is given a post in government and cannot successfully carry out his duties, and if he is sent to far places and cannot react to the circumstances as he finds them, then even if he has learnt to recite many of them, of what use is this to him?'

6. The Master said: 'If one's character is rectified, then things will get done without orders being issued; but if one's character is not rectified, then although orders are issued they are not followed.'

7. The Master said: 'The governments of Lu and Wei are as brothers.'*

8. The Master said of Prince Jing of Wei that he was skilful in his domestic arrangements. When he first had a house he said: 'It is tolerably suitable.' When he got together a few possessions, he said: 'It is more or less full.' When he had acquired luxuries, he said: 'It is reasonably attractive.'

9. When the Master went to Wei, Ran You drove his carriage. 'How dense is the population!' exclaimed the Master. 'When the people have multiplied, what more should be done for them?' said Ran You. 'Enrich them', he replied. 'And when they have been enriched, what more should be done for them?' 'Instruct them', he replied.

10. The Master said: 'If only there were someone to employ me, in not more than a year's time things would become acceptable, and after three years there would be results.'

11. The Master said: '"If good men ran a state for a hundred years, they might therefore vanquish cruelty and abolish killing." How true is this saying!'

12. The Master said: 'If there existed a true king,* after a generation humaneness would certainly prevail.'

13. The Master said: 'Suppose one rectifies one's own

character, what difficulty does one have in participating in government. If one cannot rectify one's own character, what has one to do with rectifying others?'

14. When Master Ran returned from court the Master said: 'How late you are.' He replied: 'There was government business.'* The Master said: 'If their business had included government, I would have been among those hearing about it, even though they do not employ me.'

15. Duke Ding asked if there was a single saying with which one might make a state prosperous. Master Kong replied: 'A saying cannot be quite like that. But there is a saying among men which runs "to be a ruler is difficult and to be a subject is not easy". If one understands that to be a ruler is difficult, then does this not come close to making a state prosperous through one saying?' He said: 'Is there a single saying with which one might ruin a state?' Master Kong replied: 'A saying cannot be quite like that. But there is a saying among men which runs "I have no pleasure in being a ruler, except that nobody opposes me with his words". As far as his good points are concerned, it is surely good, isn't it, that nobody opposes him? But as far as his bad points are concerned, if nobody opposes him, is this not close to ruining a state with a single saying?'

16. The Duke of She asked about government. The Master said: 'When those who are close by are pleased and those who are far off are attracted.'

17. Zixia, being prefect of Jufu, asked about government. The Master said: 'Avoid being impatient, avoid noticing minor advantages. If you are impatient, then you will not be thorough. If you notice minor advantages, then major tasks will not be accomplished.'

18. The Duke of She told Master Kong: 'In my locality there is a certain paragon, for when his father stole a sheep, he, the son, bore witness against him.' Master Kong said: 'In my locality those who are upright are different from this. Fathers cover up for their sons* and sons cover up for their fathers. Uprightness is to be found in this.'

19. Fan Chi asked about humaneness. The Master said: 'Courtesy in private life, reverence in handling business,

loyalty in relationships with others. They should not be set aside even if one visits the barbarian tribes.'

20. Zigong asked: 'What must a man be like so that he may be called a public servant?' The Master said: 'If in conducting himself he maintains a sense of honour, and if when sent to the four quarters of the world he does not disgrace his ruler's commission, he may be called a public servant.' He said: 'I venture to ask about the grade below that.' He said: 'When his relatives commend the filial piety to be found in him and his fellow-villagers commend the deference to elders he displays.' He said: 'I venture to ask about the grade below that.' He said: 'When he is always true to his word and he always brings his deeds to fruition. Although he may surprisingly appear to be a small man because of his stubbornness, on the other hand he surely may be deemed to come next.' He said: 'What about those who are at present taking part in government?' The Master said: 'Oh, why are people of such small capacity worth taking into account?'

21. The Master said: 'If one does not get hold of moderation to associate with, it is necessary to turn to either the impetuous or the cautious, is it not? But the impetuous are go-getters, and as far as the cautious are concerned, there are some things they do not do.'

22. The Master said: 'The southerners have a saying: "Without constancy a man cannot play the part of a shaman or doctor." That's good, isn't it? "If one does not show constancy* in one's virtue, one will perhaps be visited by shame."' The Master went on to say: 'They do not merely read omens.'

23. The Master said: 'The gentleman, although he behaves in a conciliatory manner, does not make his views coincide with those of others; the small man, although he makes his views coincide with those of others, does not behave in a conciliatory manner.'

24. Zigong asked: 'What about a man who is loved by all his fellow-villagers?' The Master said: 'That won't do at all.' 'And what about a man who is hated by all his fellow-villagers?' The Master said: 'That won't do at all. It would

be better if the good people among his fellow-villagers loved him and the bad people among them hated him.'

25. The Master said: 'The gentleman is easy to serve but difficult to please. If in trying to please him one does not accord with the Way, he is not pleased. But when it comes to his employing others, he takes account of their capacity. The small man is difficult to serve but easy to please. Although one does not accord with the Way when trying to please him, he is pleased. But when it comes to his employing others, he seeks perfection in them.'

26. The Master said: 'The gentleman is dignified but not arrogant. The small man is arrogant but not dignified.'

27. The Master said: 'Firmness, resoluteness, simplicity, and reticence are close to humaneness.'

28. Zilu asked: 'What must one be like so that one may be called a public servant?' The Master said: 'If one seems critical and demanding but genial, one may be called a public servant—critical and demanding among friends, but genial towards brothers.'

29. The Master said: 'Only when good men have instructed the people for seven years* may they take up arms.'

30. The Master said: 'If one fights a battle using an un-instructed people, this may be described as throwing them away.'

1.* Yuan Si asked about shame. The Master said: 'Whether the Way prevails in the state or not, to be concerned only with one's salary is shameful.'

'If one does not behave in such a way that one is domineering, boastful, resentful or covetous, one may be considered humane.' The Master said: 'It may be considered difficult, but as for humane, I do not know.'

2. The Master said: 'If although one is a public servant one cherishes staying at home, one is inadequate to perform the tasks of a public servant.'

3. The Master said: 'When the Way prevails in the state, be enterprising in speech and enterprising in action; but when the Way does not prevail in the state, be enterprising in action but prudent in speech.'

4. The Master said: 'Anyone who possesses virtue is bound to possess eloquence, but anyone who possesses eloquence does not necessarily possess virtue. Anyone who is humane is bound to possess courage, but anyone who is courageous does not necessarily possess humaneness.'

5. Nangong Kuo put a question to Master Kong: 'Yi was skilful at archery and Ao pushed a boat over dry land, but neither managed to die a natural death. Yu and Ji* personally sowed the crops but gained possession of all under Heaven.' Our Master did not reply. When Nangong Kuo went out, the Master said: 'Such a man is indeed a gentleman! Such a man does indeed honour virtue!'

6. The Master said: 'There are people who are not humane although they are gentlemen, aren't there? But there is no such thing as someone who is humane although he is a small man.'

7. The Master said: 'If one loves someone, can one avoid making him work hard? If one is loyal to someone, can one avoid instructing him?'

8. The Master said: 'When dispatches were prepared* Pi Chen roughly drafted them, Shi Shu investigated the

contents, Ziyu the official in charge of envoys amended them to cover up defects, and Zichan of Dongli embellished them.'

9. Someone asked about Zichan. The Master said: 'He was a kind man.' He asked about Zixi. The Master said: 'That man! That man!' He asked about Guan Zhong. The Master said: 'He removed from the Bo family the city of Pian with three hundred families, and though he lived on coarse rice till the end of his days, Bo* had no word of resentment.'

10. The Master said: 'To avoid resentment when one is poor is difficult, but to avoid arrogance when one is rich is easy.'

11. The Master said: 'Meng Gongchuo* would have been fine as comptroller of the Zhao and Wei houses, but he is not fit to be a grandee even in Teng or Xue.'

12. Zilu asked about the complete man.* The Master said: 'If a man is as understanding as Zang Wuzhong, as free from desires as Meng Gongchuo, as courageous as Zhuangzi of Bian, and as accomplished as Ran You, and is refined by the rites and music, then surely he may be considered a complete man.' But he went on: 'But why must the complete man of today be like this? If one thinks of what is right when one confronts advantage, if one is ready to lay down one's life when one confronts danger, and if in the case of a long-term guarantee one does not forget the words of a lifetime, one may surely be considered a complete man.'

13. The Master asked Gongming Jia about Gongshu Wenzi, saying: 'Is it true that your Master neither spoke, nor laughed, nor took?' Gongming Jia replied: 'Those who reported this were exaggerating. My Master spoke only when it was timely, so others did not weary of his speech. He laughed only when he was happy, so others did not weary of his laughter. He took only when it was right, so others did not weary of his taking.' The Master said: 'How would such behaviour be apparent?'

14. The Master said: 'Zang Wuzhong* used Fang to demand from Lu that Wei should succeed him. Even if it is said that he did not coerce his ruler, I do not believe it.'

15. The Master said: 'Duke Wen* of Jin was deceitful and

not straightforward. Duke Huan of Qi was straightforward and not deceitful.'

16.   Zilu said: 'When Duke Huan had Prince Jiu* put to death, Shao Hu died with him, but Guan Zhong did not. Shouldn't one say that he was not at all humane?' The Master said: 'The fact that, in convening the feudal lords nine times, Duke Huan did not have recourse to weapons and war-chariots is due to the efforts of Guan Zhong. But as to the question whether he was humane or not, I have nothing to say.'

17.   Zigong said: 'It is not the case that Guan Zhong was a humane person, is it? When Duke Huan had Prince Jiu put to death, Guan Zhong was unable to die and even became chief minister to him.' The Master said: 'When Guan Zhong was chief minister to Duke Huan, he became paramount leader of the feudal lords and united and restored order to all under Heaven, so that the people right up to the present enjoy the benefits he conferred. But for Guan Zhong we would be wearing our hair down and fastening our clothes on the left.* Surely this was different from the way in which the ordinary man or woman practises fidelity. If they commit suicide in a ditch, nobody is aware of it.'

18.   Grandee Zhuan, who had been an official in the household of Gongshu Wenzi, was promoted to office at court, where he joined Wenzi. When the Master heard this, he said: 'He may properly be regarded as cultured.'*

19.   The Master said that Duke Ling of Wei lacked the Way so Ji Kang Zi said: 'If he is like this then why does he not fail?' Master Kong said: 'Zhongshu Yu superintends the foreign visitors, the priest Tuo superintends the ancestral temple, and Wangsun Jia superintends the armed forces. In such circumstances why should he fail?'

20.   The Master said: 'When one is immodest in speaking about something, carrying it out is difficult.'

21.   Chen Heng assassinated Duke Jian.* After washing ceremonially Master Kong went to court and told Duke Ai, saying: 'Chen Heng has assassinated his ruler. I request that he be punished.' The Duke said: 'Tell the Three.' Master Kong said: 'Because I rank next to the grandees I dared not

fail to make a report but my lord simply says: "Tell the Three".' And when he went to the Three and told them, they forbade any action. Master Kong said: 'Because I ranked next to the grandees I dared not fail to make a report.'

22. Zilu asked about serving a ruler. The Master said: 'It means don't be deceitful. But do stand up to him.'

23. The Master said: 'The gentleman reaches out for what is above, the small man reaches out for what is below.'

24. The Master said: 'Those who studied in ancient times were doing so on their own behalf, but those who study today are doing so for the sake of others.'*

25. Qu Boyu sent someone to Master Kong. Master Kong sat with the messenger and put questions to him, saying: 'What is your master doing?' He replied: 'My master desires to reduce the number of his errors but is not yet able to do so.' When the messenger left, the Master said: 'A messenger? A messenger?'

26. When the Master said: 'If one is not in a certain office, one does not plan the governance involved in that office', Master Zeng said: 'In his thoughts a gentleman does not stray from his station.'

27. The Master said: 'The gentleman is ashamed that his words have outstripped his deeds.'

28. The Master said: 'The ways of the gentleman are three but I have no ability in them: the humane do not worry; the wise are not perplexed; and the courageous do not feel fear.' Zigong said: 'Our Master is talking about himself.'

29. When Zigong made comparisons between other people, the Master said: 'Surely Si is a man of quality, for as far as I am concerned, I don't have the time to spare.'

30. The Master said: 'One does not worry about the fact that other people do not appreciate one. One worries about the fact that one is incapable.'

31. The Master said: 'If a man does not anticipate deception and does not reckon on bad faith, but on the other hand is aware in good time when they occur, he is a man of quality, isn't he?'

32. Weisheng Mu said to Master Kong: 'Qiu,* what is all this bustling about for? Surely it is all just for the sake

of clever talk?' Master Kong said: 'It is not that I would presume to make clever talk my purpose. It is just because I detest obstinacy.'

33. The Master said: 'A fine horse is not praised for its strength, it is praised for its virtue.'

34. Someone said: 'What about "Repay hostility with kindness"?' The Master said: 'How then do you repay kindness? Repay hostility with uprightness and repay kindness with kindness.'

35. The Master said: 'Nobody understands me, do they?' Zigong said: 'Why is it that none of them understands you?' The Master said: 'I do not feel resentful towards Heaven and I do not put blame on men. But although my studies are of lowly things they reach up above, and the one that understands me will be Heaven, will it not?'

36. Gongbo Liao complained to the head of the Ji family about Zilu. Zifu Jingbo reported this, adding: 'My master certainly suffers from misunderstandings put about by Gongbo Liao, but my influence is still capable of having his corpse exposed in the market-place.' The Master said: 'Is the Way about to make progress? If so, it is due to Fate. Is the Way about to be rejected? If so, it is due to Fate. What will Gongbo Liao do as far as Fate is concerned?'

37. The Master said: 'Men of quality withdraw from their times, the next best withdraw from their place, the next best avoid looks, the next best avoid words.'

The Master said: 'There were seven men* who were active.'

38. Zilu stayed the night at Shimen. The gatekeeper said: 'Where are you from?' Zilu said: 'From the Kong family.' He said: 'That is the one who works away at it although he knows it's no good, isn't it?'

39. When the Master was playing the stone chimes in Wei, someone passed the Kong establishment carrying a basket. He said: 'To be sure he beats the chimes with feeling, doesn't he?'* Afterwards he said: 'How vulgar is he in his stubbornness. If nobody appreciates him, then he should simply give up.'

> If it is deep they get their dresses wet,
> If it is shallow they lift their skirts.

The Master said: 'That is surely decisive, but on the other hand not to treat these things as of fundamental importance is difficult.'

40.   Zizhang said: 'What is meant when the *Documents* say: "When Gao Zong* was in his mourning hut, he did not speak for three years?"' The Master said: 'Why insist on Gao Zong? The men of antiquity all did likewise. When the ruler died, for a three-year period the various ministers all combined to take orders from the chief minister.'

41.   The Master said: 'If their superior loves the rites, the people will be easy to command.'

42.   Zilu asked about the gentleman. The Master said: 'He cultivates himself in order to show reverence.' 'Is that all he does?' asked Zilu. The Master said: 'He cultivates himself so as to bring tranquillity to others.' 'Is that all he does?' Zilu again asked. The Master said: 'He cultivates himself so as to bring tranquillity to the hundred surnames. Self-cultivation so as to bring tranquillity to the hundred surnames—didn't even Yao and Shun have to take pains to achieve this?'

43.   Yuan Rang was waiting in an oafish manner. The Master said: 'When he was young he was not deferential, so when he grew up nothing was passed on by him, and now he is an old man he does not die—this seems terrible.' And he struck his shins with a stick.

44.   A boy from Que village carried messages, and someone asked whether he was the sort of person who improved. The Master said: 'I see that he sits in an adult's place and I see that he walks together with his elders. He is not the sort of person who seeks to improve. He is the sort of person who wants to get results quickly.'

BOOK 15

1. Duke Ling of Wei asked Master Kong about the deployment of troops. 'I once acquired some knowledge of the business of sacrificial vessels', replied Master Kong, 'but I have never studied military matters.' The next day he continued his journey.

2. When they were in Chen they suffered an interruption in the supply of provisions, so the followers became ill and nobody was capable of getting up. Feeling aggrieved, Zilu addressed the Master. 'Does suffering exist even for the gentleman?' he said. The Master said: 'The gentleman remains firm in the face of suffering, but if the small man suffers, he is carried away on a flood of excess.'

3. The Master said: 'Si, you think of me as one who studies many things and remembers them, don't you?' He replied: 'Yes, is it not the case?' He said: 'It is not. There is one thing* I use to string them together.'

4. The Master said: 'You, rare are those who understand virtue.'

5. The Master said: 'Surely Shun was one who governed by non-action.* For what action did he take? He merely adopted a courteous posture and faced due south.'

6. Zizhang asked about making progress. The Master said: 'If one is loyal and faithful in word and sincere and respectful in deed, then even in barbarian countries one will make progress. But if one is not loyal and faithful in word and is not sincere and respectful in deed, then will one really make progress even in one's own neighbourhood? Only if you see that these things are before you as you stand or are resting on the yoke as you sit in your carriage will you make progress.' Zizhang recorded this on his sash.

7. The Master said: 'Straight indeed was Shi Yu. When the Way prevailed in the state he was like an arrow, and when the Way did not prevail in the state he was like an arrow. A gentleman indeed was Qu Boyu. When the Way prevailed in the state, he held office; but when the Way did not prevail in

the state, then he could be rolled up so as to keep things in store.'

8. The Master said: 'Not to talk with people although they can be talked with is to waste people. To talk with people although they can't be talked with is to waste words. A man of understanding does not waste people, but he also does not waste words.'

9. The Master said: 'The determined public servant and the humane man never seek to preserve life in such a way as to injure humaneness, but they will sometimes even sacrifice their lives in order to achieve humaneness.'

10. Zigong asked about practising humaneness. The Master said: 'If he wishes to make his work good, the craftsman must first sharpen his tools. If one is staying in a particular state, one serves the people of highest quality among its grandees and makes friends with the most humane among its public servants.'

11. Yan Hui asked about governing a state. The Master said: 'Introduce the seasons of Xia, ride the state carriage of Yin, wear the ceremonial cap of Zhou. For music adopt the *shao* and *wu*. Get rid of the sounds of Zheng,* and banish clever talkers. The sounds of Zheng are licentious and clever talkers are a menace.'

12. The Master said: 'If a man avoids thinking about distant matters he will certainly have worries close at hand.'

13. The Master said: 'It is no good! I have never come across anyone who admires virtue as much as he admires sexual attraction.'

14. The Master said: 'Surely Zang Wenzhong was a person who stole position. He knew the qualities of Liu Xia Hui,* but did not give him position.'

15. The Master said: 'If one demands much from oneself and places little responsibility on others, then one will keep discontent at bay.'

16. The Master said: 'I can do nothing at all for someone who does not say "what shall I do about this, what shall I do about this?"'

17. The Master said: 'It is surely difficult for a group of people to spend a whole day on their fondness for per-

forming trivial acts of cleverness without their conversation turning to questions of right and wrong.'

18. The Master said: 'Righteousness the gentleman regards as the essential stuff and the rites are his means of putting it into effect. If modesty is the quality with which he reveals it and good faith is his method of bringing it to completion, he is indeed a gentleman.'

19. The Master said: 'The gentleman is pained at the lack of ability within himself; he is not pained at the fact that others do not appreciate him.'

20. The Master said: 'The gentleman would be upset at the idea of his reputation* not being praised after his death.'

21. The Master said: 'What the gentleman seeks in himself the small man seeks in others.'

22. The Master said: 'Gentlemen are proud but not quarrelsome. They are sociable but do not form parties.'*

23. The Master said: 'Gentlemen do not promote someone because of what he says, and do not reject what is said because of who said it.'

24. Zigong asked: 'Is there a single word such that one could practise it throughout one's life?' The Master said: 'Reciprocity perhaps? Do not inflict on others what you yourself would not wish done to you.'

25. The Master said: 'In my relationship with others whom have I blamed and whom have I praised? If there is anyone I have praised, there is surely something which I have taken as a criterion. Indeed it is the people round about who are the reason why the three dynasties* have acted in accordance with the straightforward Way.'

26.* The Master said: 'I am just about as good as a clerk with gaps in his refinement. Those who had horses lent them to others to drive them, and now surely such people no longer exist.'

27. The Master said: 'Clever words upset virtue. If one is intolerant in minor matters, one upsets major plans.'

28. The Master said: 'When the multitude hate somebody, it is necessary to look into his case; and when the multitude love somebody, it is necessary to look into his case.'

29. The Master said: 'Man can enlarge the Way, but it is not true that the Way enlarges man.'

30. The Master said: 'If one commits an error and does not reform, this is what is meant by an error.'

31. The Master said: 'I once did not eat all day and did not sleep all night in order to think, but there was no benefit. It would have been better to study.'

32. The Master said: 'The gentleman plans for the Way and does not plan for food. If you plough, hunger is a possible outcome; but if you study, official salary is a possible outcome. So the gentleman is concerned about the Way and is not concerned about poverty.'

33. The Master said: 'If knowledge attains something but humaneness cannot safeguard it, then one is bound to lose it even if one has got hold of it. If knowledge attains something and humaneness can safeguard it and if one does not govern them with dignity, then the people will not be respectful. If knowledge attains something and humaneness can safeguard it and if one governs them with dignity, but if in moving them into action one does not accord with the rites, one is not yet good.'

34. The Master said: 'The gentleman cannot be appreciated in minor matters, but can be accepted in major matters. The small man cannot be accepted in major matters, but can be appreciated in minor matters.'

35. The Master said: 'The people's connection with humaneness is more important than water or fire. As for water and fire, I have come across people who have died through stepping on them, but I have never come across people who have died through stepping on humaneness.'

36. The Master said: 'When one is confronted by humaneness, one does not yield precedence to one's teacher.'

37. The Master said: 'The gentleman is correct but not inflexible.'

38. The Master said: 'In serving one's ruler one deals reverently with the tasks involved and makes the livelihood involved a secondary consideration.'

39. The Master said: 'If there is instruction there is no categorization.'*

40. The Master said: 'If their Ways are not the same, people do not make plans for them together.'

41. The Master said: 'In words the purpose is simply to get one's point across.'

42. Music-master* Mian called and, when they reached the steps, the Master said: 'Here are the steps.' When they reached the mat, the Master said: 'Here is the mat.' When they all sat down, the Master informed him: 'So and so is there, so and so is there.' After music-master Mian had left Zizhang asked: 'Is speaking about such things with music-masters in accordance with the Way?' The Master said: 'Yes, that is certainly the way to assist a music-master.'

BOOK 16

1. The head of the Ji family was about to attack Zhuanyu.*
Ran You and Zilu, when they were received by Master
Kong, said: 'The head of the Ji family is about to take action
against Zhuanyu.' Master Kong said: 'Qiu, surely this is your
fault? As for Zhuanyu, in ancient times the former kings put
it in charge of the sacrifice to Mount Dongmeng. Moreover it
is within the frontiers of our state. This place is a servant of
the altars of land and grain, so why should it be attacked?'
Ran You said: 'Our master desires this, but neither of us two
ministers is in favour.' Master Kong said: 'Qiu, among the
sayings of Zhou Ren there is one which goes: "When you
deploy your strength and make people join the ranks, the
incompetent should drop out, for what use will those
assistants be who do not provide support when there is
danger and do not prop people up when they totter?"
Moreover your words are mistaken. When a tiger or a
rhinoceros gets out of a cage, or tortoise-shell or jade are
damaged in a box, whose fault is it?' Ran You said: 'At
present Zhuanyu is strong and it is close to Bi. If it is not
taken now, in later generations it is bound to become a
source of anxiety to his sons and grandsons.' Master Kong
said: 'Qiu, the gentleman detests the refusal to say outright
that one wants something while making a point of arguing
in favour of it. I have heard that the possessors of states or
noble families do not worry about underpopulation, but
worry about the people being unevenly distributed; do not
worry about poverty, but worry about discontent. For when
there is even distribution there is no poverty, and when there
is harmony there is no underpopulation, and when there is
contentment there will be no upheavals.* It is for such
reasons that, if far-off people do not submit, then culture
and virtue are enhanced in order to attract them; and when
they have been attracted, they will be made content. Now as
far as you two are concerned, when you assist your master,
the far-off people do not submit and he is unable to attract

them. The state is divided and in a condition of collapse, split and disintegrating and he is unable to preserve it. Instead you plan to wield dagger-axe and shield within the state. I am afraid that the sorrows of the head of the Ji family do not reside in Zhuanyu, but within his own walls.'

2. Master Kong said: 'When the Way prevails in all under Heaven, the rites, music, and punitive expeditions emanate from the Son of Heaven. When the Way does not prevail in all under Heaven, then the rites, music, and punitive expeditions emanate from the feudal lords. If they emanate from the feudal lords, surely it is rare for them not to be lost* within ten generations; and if they emanate from their grandees, it is rare for them not to be lost within five generations. If their subordinate officials have control of state commands, it is rare for them not to be lost within three generations. When the Way prevails in all under Heaven, government is not in the hands of the grandees. When the Way prevails in all under Heaven, ordinary people do not hold discussions.'

3. Master Kong said: 'It is five generations since state revenues left the control of the ducal house and it is four generations since the government passed into the hands of the grandees, so the descendants of the three Huan* have gone into decline.'

4. Master Kong said: 'There are three kinds of friendship which are beneficial and three kinds of friendship which are harmful. It is beneficial to make friends with the upright, to make friends with the sincere, and to make friends with those who have heard many things. It is harmful to make friends with the ingratiating, to make friends with those who are good at seeming pliant, and to make friends with those who have a ready tongue.'

5. Master Kong said: 'There are three kinds of pleasure which are beneficial and three kinds of pleasure which are harmful. It is beneficial to take pleasure in the proper arrangement of rites and music, to take pleasure in talking about the good points of other men, to take pleasure in having a large number of friends who are men of quality. It is harmful to take pleasure in the delights of showing off,

to take pleasure in a self-indulgent life-style, and to take pleasure in the delights of feasting.'

6. Master Kong said: 'When in attendance on a gentleman there are three mistakes which may be made: to speak when it is not yet time for one to speak is called presumptuousness; not to speak when it is time for one to speak is called secretiveness; to speak when one has not yet observed his expression is called blindness.'

7. Master Kong said: 'There are three things which the gentleman guards against: in the time of his youth, when his vital powers have not yet settled down, he is on his guard in matters of sex; when he reaches the prime of life and his vital powers have just attained consistency, he is on his guard in matters of contention; and when he becomes old and his vital powers have declined, he is on his guard in matters of acquisition.'

8. Master Kong said: 'There are three things which the gentleman holds in awe: he is in awe of the decree of Heaven, he is in awe of great men, and he is in awe of the words of sages. The small man, being unaware of the decree of Heaven, is not in awe of it. He is rude to great men and ridicules the words of sages.'

9. Master Kong said: 'Those who know things from birth come first; those who know things from study come next; those who study things although they find them difficult come next to them; and those who do not study because they find things difficult, that is to say the common people, come last.'

10. Master Kong said: 'There are nine things the gentleman concentrates on: in seeing he concentrates on clarity, in listening he concentrates on acuteness, in expression he concentrates on warmness, in demeanour he concentrates on courtesy, in words he concentrates on loyalty, in deeds he concentrates on reverence, when he is in doubt he concentrates on asking questions, when he is indignant he concentrates on the problems, and when he sees opportunity for gain he concentrates on what is right.'

11. Master Kong said: ' "Seeing good he behaves as if he will not attain it, and seeing what is not good he behaves as

if he is testing hot water." I have met such people and I have heard such a saying. "He lives in retirement in order to seek to attain his purpose, and he does what is right in order to spread the influence of his Way." I have heard such a saying but I have never met such people.'

12.   Duke Jing of Qi possessed a thousand teams of four horses, but on the day he died the people had no opportunity to offer him praise.* Bo Yi and Shu Qi starved at the foot of Mount Shouyang and the people praise them right up to the present. Surely the saying* applies to these men.

13.   Ziqin asked Boyu:* 'Being his son you surely received special instruction?' He replied: 'Never. He was once standing by himself when I crossed the courtyard hurriedly* and he said: "Are you studying the *Songs*?" When I replied: "Not yet", he went on: "If you do not study the *Songs*, you will have nothing to talk about." So I went away and studied the *Songs*. On another day he was also standing by himself when I crossed the courtyard hurriedly, and he said: "Are you studying the rites?" When I replied: "Not yet", he went on: "If you do not study the rites, you will have no way of taking your stand." So I went away and studied the rites. I received these two pieces of instruction.' Ziqin went away and said with delight: 'I put one question and got three answers. I heard about the *Songs*, I heard about the rites, and I also heard that the gentleman keeps his son at a distance.'

14.*   The wife of a lord of a state is referred to by the lord as 'the lady'. She refers to herself as 'little child'. The people of the state refer to her as 'the lord's lady', and when they refer to her in communication with other states, they call her 'our lesser lord', and when people of other states refer to her, they also call her 'the lord's lady'.

BOOK 17

1. Yang Huo wished to see Master Kong, but Master Kong did not see him, so he sent Master Kong a piglet. Master Kong, choosing a time when he would be absent from home, went to pay his respects to him. But Yang met him on the road. He said to Master Kong: 'Come here, I've got something to say to you.' He went on: 'If one hugs one's treasure* close so that one is letting one's country go astray, can one be called humane? No, one cannot. If one longs to take part in affairs, but regularly misses the opportunity, can one be called understanding? No, one cannot. The days and months slip by, and the years are not on our side.' 'All right', said Master Kong. 'I shall take office.'

2. The Master said: 'By nature close to each other,* but through practice far apart from each other.'

The Master said: 'Only the most intelligent and the most stupid do not change.'

3. When the Master went to Wucheng, he heard the sound of strings and singing. Smiling broadly, our Master said: 'Why use an ox-knife* to cut a chicken?' Ziyou replied: 'Once upon a time I heard from you the remark that, when a gentleman studies the Way, he loves his fellow-men; and when a small man studies the Way, he is easy to command.' The Master said: 'My friends, his words are true. What I said just now was only joking about it.'

4. Gongshan Furao carried out a rebellion using Bi as his base. He sent for the Master, who wanted to go. Zilu was displeased. 'There is absolutely no question of going there', he said. 'Why make a point of going to Gongshan.' The Master said: 'The man who sends for me surely does not do so pointlessly. If there were anyone who would employ me, I would make a Zhou in the East,* wouldn't I?'

5. Zizhang asked Master Kong about humaneness. Master Kong said: 'One who can bring about the practice of five things everywhere under Heaven has achieved humaneness. When he begged to ask about them, he said: 'Courtesy,

tolerance, good faith, diligence, and kindness. If one is courteous, one is not treated with rudeness; if one is tolerant, one wins over the multitude; if one is of good faith, others give one responsibility; if one is diligent, one obtains results; and if one is kind, one is competent to command others.'

6. When Bi Xi sent for him, the Master wanted to go. Zilu said: 'Master, I once heard the following from you: "If someone in his own person does those things which are not good, the gentleman does not enter his domain." Bi Xi is carrying out a rebellion using Zhongmou as his base, so what is the point of your going there?' The Master said: 'Yes, I have said such a thing, but is it not said that "hard indeed is that which is not worn thin by grinding" and "white indeed is that which will not turn black from dyeing"? Surely I am not just a bitter gourd!* How can I hang there and not be eaten?'

7. The Master said: 'You, have you heard the six sayings about the six hidden consequences?' When he replied that he had not, the Master went on: 'Sit down and I will tell you. If one loves humaneness but does not love learning, the consequence of this is folly; if one loves understanding but does not love learning, the consequence of this is unorthodoxy; if one loves good faith but does not love learning, the consequence of this is damaging behaviour; if one loves straightforwardness but does not love learning, the consequence of this is rudeness; if one loves courage but does not love learning, the consequence of this is rebelliousness; if one loves strength but does not love learning, the consequence of this is violence.'

8. The Master said: 'My young friends, why do none of you study the *Songs*? The *Songs* may help one to be stimulated, to observe, to be sociable, and to express grievances. One uses them at home to serve one's father, and one uses them in distant places to serve one's ruler. One also gains much knowledge concerning the names of birds and beasts and plants and trees.'

The Master said to Boyu: 'Have you done the *Zhounan* and *Shaonan*?* If although one is a man one has not done the *Zhounan* and *Shaonan*, surely it is like standing with one's face to the wall?'

9. The Master said: 'When one talks repeatedly of ritual,* does one really only mean jades and silk? When one talks repeatedly of music, does one really only mean bells and drums?'

10. The Master said: 'If one is outwardly fierce but inwardly feeble, one may be compared to the small man. In fact isn't one just like a burglar making a hole through a wall?'

11. The Master said: 'The village worthy* is the spoiler of virtue.'

12. The Master said: 'To listen on the highway and then talk in the byways constitutes the rejection of virtue.'*

13. The Master said: 'Is it really possible to serve one's ruler alongside vulgar persons? For while they have not yet obtained something, they are worried about obtaining it; and when they have obtained it, they are worried about losing it. And if they are worried about losing it, there are no lengths to which they will not go.'

14. The Master said: 'In ancient times the people had three weaknesses, but now perhaps these have been lost. The impetuosity of antiquity led to recklessness, but the impetuosity of today results in licentiousness; the pride of antiquity meant that people were incorruptible, but the pride of today means that people are quarrelsome and irritable; the simple-mindedness of antiquity resulted in straightforwardness, but the simple-mindedness of today is merely artfulness.'

15. The Master said: 'Clever words and a plausible appearance have seldom turned out to be humane.'

16. The Master said: 'I hate the fact that purple is displacing vermilion,* I hate the fact that the sounds of Zheng* are ruining elegant music, and I hate the fact that sharp tongues are subverting states and families.'

17. The Master said: 'I wish to do without speech.' Zigong said: 'If you do not speak, what will be handed on by your disciples?' The Master said: 'What ever does Heaven say?* Yet the four seasons run their course through it and all

things are produced by it. What ever does Heaven say?'

18. Ru Bei wished to see Master Kong. Master Kong declined and made illness the pretext. When the man who brought the message went out of the door, he took up his zithern and sang, and made sure that he heard it.

19. Zai Wo asked about the three years' mourning,* since one year was already long enough. 'If gentlemen do not practise the rites for three years', he said, 'the rites will certainly decay. If they do not make music for three years, music will certainly die. The old crops have gone and the new crops have come up and the drills have made new fire,* so after a completed year the mourning should stop.' The Master said: 'If you were then to eat good rice and wear embroidered clothes, would you feel at ease?' 'Yes', he replied. 'If you would be at ease, then do so', said the Master. 'But when a gentleman is in mourning, if he eats dainties he does not relish them, and if he hears music he does not enjoy it, and if he sits in his usual place he is not at ease. That is why he abstains from these things. But if you feel at ease, then do them!' When Zai Wo had left, the Master said: 'As for Yu's inhumaneness, it is not until a child is three years old that it escapes from being nursed by its parents. The three years' mourning is the mourning universally adopted by all under Heaven. Surely Yu had three years' love from his parents?'

20. The Master said: 'It is surely difficult to spend the whole day stuffing oneself with food and having nothing to use one's mind on. Are there not people who play *bo* and *yi*?* Even such activity is definitely superior, is it not?'

21. Zilu said: 'Does the gentleman esteem courage?' The Master said: 'Rightness the gentleman regards as paramount; for if a gentleman has courage but lacks a sense of right and wrong, he will cause political chaos; and if a small man has courage but lacks a sense of right and wrong, he will commit burglary.'

22. Zigong said: 'Does the gentleman also have hatreds?' The Master said: 'He has. He hates those who proclaim what is hateful in others; he hates those who, since they occupy inferior positions, revile those who are superior to them; he

hates those who are courageous but do without the rites; he hates those who are determined and daring but obstructive. Do you also have hatreds?' Zigong said: 'I hate those who treat investigation as understanding, I hate those who treat insubordination as courage, and I hate those who treat talebearing as honesty.'

23. The Master said: 'Only women* and small men seem difficult to look after. If you keep them close, they become insubordinate; but if you keep them at a distance, they become resentful.'

24. The Master said: 'If hateful things are seen in one at the age of forty, that is indeed how one will end up.'

BOOK 18

1. The Viscount of Wei fled from him,* the Viscount of Ji became a slave because of him, and Bi Gan remonstrated and met his death. The Master said: 'In the Yin there were three humane men.'

2. When Liu Xia Hui was leader of the public servants, he was dismissed three times. 'Should you not go away?' said someone. He said: 'If I serve others in an honest way, where shall I go and not be dismissed three times? If I served men in a crooked way, what need would there be for me to leave the country of my parents?'

3. When Duke Jing of Qi received Master Kong he said: 'If it is a question of treating him like the Ji family, I cannot do so.' He received him in a manner midway between that accorded to the Ji and the Meng.* He said: 'I have grown old and am unable to offer employment.' Master Kong left.

4. The men of Qi made a present of female entertainers. Ji Huan Zi* accepted them and did not attend court for three days. Master Kong left.

5. Jie Yu, the madman of Chu, passed Master Kong, singing:

> Phoenix, phoenix,
> What a decline of virtue!
> What is past is beyond reproof,
> Though what is to come may still be pursued.
> Have done, have done,
> For those who engage in government today
>   are in peril.

Master Kong got down and wished to speak with him. But he hurried off and avoided him, so that he did not succeed in speaking with him.

6. Changju and Jieni were ploughing as a team together. When Master Kong passed them, he got Zilu to ask them about a ford. Changju said: 'Who is that person in charge of the carriage?' Zilu said: 'It is Kong Qiu.' He said: 'Is that

Kong Qiu of Lu?' He said that it was. He said: 'That one already knows the way across.'* He then put the question to Jieni, who asked who he was. He said: 'I am Zilu.' 'Is that the disciple of Kong Qiu of Lu?' he said. 'Yes', he replied. He said: 'A rushing torrent, that's all the world is, and who has the means to change it? Moreover instead of following a chap who avoids other people, would it not be better to follow a chap who shuns his whole generation?' And he did not stop ploughing. Zilu went and reported this. His Master spoke vaguely and absent-mindedly. 'One cannot flock with birds and beasts', he said. 'If I am not to be an associate of such men as these, with whom am I to associate? But if the Way prevailed in all under Heaven, I would not change places with him.'*

7. Once when in his company Zilu fell behind. He met an old man carrying a basket on a staff. 'Have you seen our Master, sir?', said Zilu. The old man said: 'Your four limbs do not toil, and the five grains you cannot tell apart. Who is your Master?' He planted his staff on the ground and began weeding. Zilu stood by with his hands respectfully held together. He made Zilu stay and spend the night. Having killed a chicken and prepared millet, he gave him a meal and presented his two sons to him. Next day Zilu went on his way and reported this. 'He is a recluse', said the Master, and sent Zilu back to see him again; but when he got there he had gone. Zilu said: 'Not to hold an official position shows a lack of a sense of duty. If the rules which govern the relationship between old and young cannot be set aside, why should the duty which binds ruler and subject be set aside? Wishing to preserve the purity of his own character, he spoils the most important of human relationships. When a gentleman holds office, he performs the duties which belong to it. That the Way is not practised he is already aware.'

8.* People who retired from the world: Bo Yi, Shu Qi, Yu Zhong, Yi Yi, Zhu Zhang, Liu Xia Hui, Shao Lian. The Master said: 'They did not allow their resolve to weaken and did not allow their persons to be humiliated—surely this describes Bo Yi and Shu Qi. This means that although Liu Xia Hui and Shao Lian did allow their resolve to weaken, and did allow their persons to be humiliated, their words were consonant with their obligations and their deeds were consonant with their reflections—precisely that. It means that Yu Zhong and Yi Yi lived as recluses but were free of speech and, while they succeeded in being incorruptible in their personal lives, they also maintained authority when they were dismissed. As for me, I am different from these. I avoid saying what should or should not be done.'

9. The grand music-master Zhi went to Qi. Gan, leader of the second course, went to Chu. Liao, leader of the third course, went to Cai. Que, leader of the fourth course, went to Qin. The drummer Fang Shu crossed the Ho. Wu, player of the hand-drum, crossed the Han. Assistant music-master Yang and Xiang, player of the stone-chimes, crossed the sea.

10. The Duke of Zhou said to the Duke of Lu: 'The gentleman does not neglect his relations, and does not cause his chief officials to feel resentful at their advice not being taken. If there is no important reason, officials of long standing are not cast out; and he avoids seeking perfection in one man.'

11. In Zhou there were eight public servants: Bo Da, Bo Kuo, Zhong Tu, Zhong Hu, Shu Ye, Shu Xia, Ji Sui, and Ji Kuo.

BOOK 19

1   Zizhang said: 'A public servant who on confronting danger is prepared to lay down his life, who on confronting gain concentrates on what is right, who when sacrificing concentrates on reverence, who when mourning concentrates on grief should definitely be all right.'

2.   Zizhang said: 'If someone grasps hold of virtue but does not hold it firmly and believes in the Way but is not convinced, how can he be regarded as possessing them and how can he be regarded as not possessing them?'

3.   The disciples of Zixia asked Zizhang about relationships. Zizhang said: 'What does Zixia say?' They replied: 'Zixia says: "Associate with those with whom it is proper to associate, and reject those with whom it is not proper to associate."' Zizhang said: 'That is different from what I have heard: a gentleman, while honouring men of quality, tolerates the multitude; and, while praising the good, pities the incapable. If I have great qualities, then whom among men do I not tolerate? And if I am not a man of quality, then people will reject me; so in that case how shall I reject others?'

4.   Zixia said: 'Even lesser arts are bound to have something noteworthy in them, but if they are taken too far, there is a fear that one could get stuck in the mud, and that is why the gentleman does not practise them.'

5.   Zixia said: 'If day by day one is aware of what one lacks, but month by month never forgets what one is capable of, one may definitely be said to be fond of learning.'

6.   Zixia said: 'If one studies widely and is sincere in one's purpose, and if one enquires earnestly and reflects on what is at hand, then humaneness is to be found among such activities.'

7.   Zixia said: 'The various craftsmen occupy workshops in order to complete their tasks, but the gentleman studies in order to develop his Way.'

8.   Zixia said: 'The errors of a small man are always glossed over.'

9.   Zixia said: 'The gentleman undergoes three transformations: when one sees him from a distance he is rather forbidding, but when one approaches him he is genial, and then when one listens to his words they are strict.'

10.   Zixia said: 'The gentleman wins the people's trust before subjecting them to hard work; for if he has not yet won their trust, they will think he is treating them harshly. He wins his superior's trust before remonstrating with him; for if he has not yet won his trust, the superior will think that he is disparaging him.'

11.   Zixia said: 'So long as one does not cross the barrier in the matter of greater virtue, it is permissible to ignore it with regard to lesser virtue.'

12.   Ziyou said: 'At sprinkling and sweeping, responding and replying, advancing and retiring Zixia's disciples and young followers are all right. But these are the branches, and it is the root which they lack, so what should be done about them?' When Zixia heard this, he said: 'Alas, Ziyou is wrong. In the Way of the gentleman what does one transmit first, and what does one put last and treat more casually? Like the various plants and trees, these things are separated off according to their differences. How can the Way of the gentleman be so falsely represented? Surely it is only the sage who embraces both beginning and end?'*

13.   Zixia said: 'If one has more than enough energy for office, then one studies; and if one has more than enough energy for study, then one holds office.'

14.   Ziyou said: 'Mourning stops when it has caught up with grief.'

15.   Ziyou said: 'My friend Zizhang seems hard to emulate, but he is not yet humane.'

16.   Master Zeng said: 'Magnificent indeed is Zizhang, but it is difficult to collaborate with him in the practice of humaneness.'

17.   Master Zeng said: 'I heard this from our Master: "People who have fully extended themselves have never existed, yet it is necessary to do so in the mourning of parents, isn't it?"'

18.   Master Zeng said: 'I have heard this from our Master: "The filial piety of Meng Zhuang Zi people may be capable of in other respects, but as for his not altering his father's officials at the same time as his father's governance—this is difficult to be able to do."'

19.   The Meng family appointed Yang Fu to be leader of the public servants, so he put questions to Master Zeng. Master Zeng said: 'For a long time those in authority have lost their Way and the people have become disorganized. If you get hold of the truth of the matter, show sadness and pity, and do not feel pleased about it.'

20.   Zigong said: 'Zhou's* wickedness was not as extreme as this. That is why the gentleman hates to dwell downstream, where the evils of all under Heaven accumulate.'

21.   Zigong said: 'The errors of the gentleman are like eclipses of the sun and moon. When he errs everyone observes him; and when he makes a correction, everyone looks up to him.'

22.   Gongsun Chao of Wei asked Zigong: 'From whom did Zhongni* derive his learning?' Zigong said: 'The Way of Kings Wen and Wu has not yet collapsed to the ground. It is here present among us, and men of quality remember its more important principles, and those who are not men of quality remember its less important principles. So everyone has the Way of Wen and Wu within himself. From whom then does the Master not learn, and yet what regular teacher does he have?'

23.   Shusun Wushu said to the grandees at court: 'Zigong is superior to Zhongni.' Zifu Jingbo reported this to Zigong, who said: 'Compare this with the wall surrounding a building. My wall reaches shoulder height, and if one peers over it one sees the good qualities of the house. But our Master's wall is several *ren** high, and if one does not find the gate in it so as to enter, one does not see the beauty of the ancestral temple and the sumptuousness of the various official departments. Those who have found the gate in it have presumably been few, so is it not therefore only to be expected that that gentleman should say such a thing?'

24.   When Shusun Wushu slandered Zhongni, Zigong said: 'There is no point in doing so. Zhongni cannot be slandered.

The most outstanding among other men are as hills and mounds, for they can still be climbed over. But Zhongni is as the sun or moon, for there is no possibility of climbing over him. Even if people wished to cut themselves off from them, what harm would this do to the sun or the moon? It would just go to show all the more clearly that they did not understand how to measure.'

25.   Chen Ziqin said to Zigong: 'You are being polite. Zhongni is surely not more outstanding than you.' Zigong said: 'For a single saying a gentleman may be considered wise and for a single saying he may be considered unwise, so words simply must be used with care. The fact that our Master is beyond reach is just like the fact that Heaven cannot be climbed by stairs. If our Master got control of a state or a great family, then, as the saying* goes, "When he set them up, they were established; when he led them on their way, they went; when he comforted them, they came to him; when he brought them into action, they worked in harmony. In his life he was glorious and in his death he was lamented." Surely he is beyond reach?'

BOOK 20

1.* Yao said: 'Ah, Shun, the heavenly succession is upon thine own person, so grasp it firmly and with all sincerity. If there is dire distress within the four seas, the Heaven-sent favours will be terminated for ever.' Shun also charged Yu with these words.

Tang said: 'I, this little child, venture to offer a black male victim, and venture to make manifest this declaration before the august sovereign lord that those who have transgressed I dare not pardon, but thy servants, O God, I will not hide, so that the choice lies in thine own heart. If I in mine own person have transgressed, let not the guilt be transferred to the people of the myriad regions, but if the people of the myriad regions have transgressed, may their crime be upon me alone.'

Zhou possessed great blessings and good men it enriched. 'But even although I have close kin, it is best to have good men, and if the hundred surnames have done wrong, it shall be upon me alone.'

He paid careful attention to weights and measures, investigated the laws and regulations, re-established discarded departments of state, and government throughout the four quarters was carried out through this. He restored countries that had been wiped out, revived lines of succession which had been broken and promoted people who had become estranged, and the people of all under Heaven gave back their hearts through this. What he most stressed was people, food, mourning, sacrifices. Since he was tolerant, he won over the multitude. Since he was of good faith, the people gave him responsibility. Since he was diligent, he obtained results. Since he was just, they were pleased.

2. Zizhang asked Master Kong: 'What sort of person must one be so that one may take part in government?' 'If one honours the five excellences and puts away the four abominations, one may take part in government', said the Master. 'What is meant by the five excellences?' said

Zizhang. Master Kong said: 'When the gentleman is not wasteful although he is bounteous, when he is not resented although he gets people to work hard, when he is not greedy although he has desires, when he is not arrogant although he is dignified, when he is not fearsome although he is awe-inspiring.' 'What is meant by not being wasteful although one is bounteous?' said Zizhang. Master Kong said: 'If he benefits the people on the basis of what the people will really find beneficial, then surely he is not wasteful although he is bounteous. If he gets people to work hard by choosing tasks which may properly be worked hard at, then who will feel resentful? If through desiring humaneness, he gets humaneness, then how is he being greedy? No matter whether he is dealing with the multitude or with the few, with the small or with the great, if the gentleman never ventures to be rude, then surely he is not arrogant although he is dignified. When the gentleman adjusts his clothes and cap and makes the people gaze on him with honour, and men look upon him in dread because of his majestic appearance, surely he is not fearsome although he is awe-inspiring?' 'What is meant by the four abominations?' said Zizhang. The Master said: 'To impose the death penalty without people previously being given any instruction is called ruthlessness. To look to the completion of tasks without giving notice in advance is called harshness. To insist on a time limit although dilatory in giving orders is called oppressiveness. And generally speaking in dealing with people, niggardliness in giving is called officiousness.'

3. The Master said: 'If one does not understand fate, one has no means of becoming a gentleman; if one does not understand the rites, one has no means of taking one's stand; if one does not understand words, one has no means of understanding people.'

EXPLANATORY NOTES

THESE notes are intended to explain obscurities and also to point out passages which are of seminal importance for the history of Confucianism. The words 'Confucian' and 'Confucianism' are used in the notes to refer not to an institutionalized religion, but to the tendency to think and behave in a manner derived not simply from the words of Master Kong in the *Analects*, but to other ancient works associated with his name. Other systems of belief such as Buddhism and Daoism were also, like Confucianism, diffused throughout Chinese society, although Confucianism gained particular influence with the intellectuals because of the use of texts associated with the Master in the civil service examinations. Names of people and places are included if it is important to know their identity. If not, they may be found in the index.

1.2 *Master You*: You Ruo is generally referred to as Master You, and he makes his own pronouncements instead of merely putting questions to Master Kong. Clearly he was a teacher in the Confucian tradition.

civil disorder: this sentence is an expression of what later became the standard Confucian view that the political virtues of obedience and loyalty are family virtues writ large.

1.4 *Master Zeng*: he is always referred to thus and was clearly a prominent teacher in the early Confucian movement. He is depicted as a conscientious man, as this saying indicates, and is especially associated with the virtue of filial piety. Indeed he is presented as Master Kong's interlocutor in the *Book of Filial Piety*. Because You and Zeng are referred to as Master You and Master Zeng, there is a theory that the *Analects* was compiled by their pupils.

1.5 *country of a thousand chariots*: this is a conventional way of referring to a large state capable of putting such a force into the field.

economical in expenditure: this is not only a Confucian ideal. It is also the name of one of the chapters in the *Mo Zi*, a book purporting to contain the ideas of the fifth-century philosopher Mo Di. 'Employing the people in due season' is a common theme in the *Mencius*: the peasants should not be taken off the land at vital times during the agricultural year to work on luxuries for their rulers.

1.7 *Zixia*: a disciple who features prominently in the *Analects*, in which he appears to be particularly interested in study.

1.10 *Zigong*: one of the best-known of Master Kong's disciples, he is mentioned many times in the *Analects*. He had a distinguished career both as a diplomat and as a merchant.

1.11 *filial*: the proponents of the oppressive type of filial piety found in later China could take this chapter as authority.

1.12 *ritual*: the purpose of ritual (*li*) is to bring about harmony between man and nature, but it is no use seeking such harmony if you do not do so in conformity with the proper ritual.

1.15 *the Way*: this word preserves the parallelism and occurs in one version of the text, so it seems best to include it.

Songs: the *Book of Songs* was often quoted in antiquity to support an argument, but as here the context of the quotation could be ignored in order to make the point. In the original the words are used to describe the elegance of a young prince, but here they are taken as a simile for moral self-improvement and, as such, are commended by Master Kong. At the end of the chapter the Master refers to the quickness of uptake necessary to be proficient in the use of the *Songs*.

Si: this is Zigong's personal name. The Master normally refers to or addresses his disciples by their personal name, which reflects the familiarity appropriate to the relationship.

2.1 *pole-star*: this chapter is reminiscent of Daoist government by inactivity rather than the more interventionist philosophy of Confucianism, although later Confucian thought did see a cosmic role for the virtuous ruler.

2.2 *let there be no depravity in your thoughts*: the quotation in fact comes from a description of horses, and the words taken here to mean 'no depravity' meant 'without swerving' in the original context; while the word rendered as 'thoughts' did not carry that sense, but was merely used as an exclamation. (Since 'thoughts' is the normal *Analects* meaning of the word, it has generally been assumed by translators that that is the sense given to it here.)

2.4   *at seventy*: this is one of the most famous sayings of Master Kong, but it is not easy to interpret the various stages. Finally as a result of the process of self-cultivation and the internalization of moral values he eventually attains the unthinking adoption of moral standards. The authenticity of the chapter has been regarded as suspect both because of its self-satisfaction and because of its polished style, although Hall and Ames in *Thinking Through Confucius* are so confident of its authenticity that they use the items as themes of the separate sections of their book.

2.5   *Meng Yi Zi*: head of one of the three powerful families who had usurped authority in the state of Lu. He was succeeded by his son Meng Wu Bo, who is mentioned in the next chapter.

2.7   *Ziyou*: one of the younger disciples of Master Kong who is credited with sayings of his own in later chapters of the *Analects*.

2.9   *Hui*: Yan Hui, Master Kong's favourite pupil, admirable for his love of learning and virtuous conduct despite extreme poverty. His early death greatly saddened the Master. This first reference to him, however, seems to suggest that he does not always show sufficient independence of mind for the Master's taste.

2.12   *implement*: this important saying puts in a nutshell the belief that the gentleman's training should not be confined to particular skills so that he may become the tool or implement of others. It must instead develop his moral qualities and powers of leadership. Thus in the later Empire the traditional Chinese education for government service was concerned with the study of Confucian writings rather than with the acquisition of techniques.

2.16   *16*: the sense of this chapter is obscure and controversial. In conformist late imperial times it could conveniently be taken to mean 'if one applies oneself to unorthodox issues, it is indeed damaging.'

2.17   *You*: the personal name of the well-known disciple Zilu, whose character shines clearly through this motley collection of sayings and anecdotes. He was an extrovert man of action and not very fond of learning. Often the exchanges between Zilu and Master Kong, brief though they are, shed an amusing light on the character of Zilu and the Master's attitude towards him.

2.19 *Duke Ai*: ruler of Lu between 494 and 468. The actual power was in the hands of the Three Families, so presumably this was said when he was planning to try to regain power.

2.20 *Ji Kang Zi*: head of one of the Three Families and hereditary chief minister and effectively ruler in Lu from 492 to 468.

2.21 *Book of Documents*: this is a quotation from a lost section of the *Book of Documents*, an ancient text later incorporated in the Confucian Classics. We cannot tell, but it seems likely that Master Kong is using the words out of context to support his view that the practice of family virtues makes its own contribution to the political process.

2.22 *yoking horses*: the text in fact specifies the parts essential to the operation of small and large carriages, but I have avoided these technicalities in my translation. The analogy means that good faith is an essential ingredient of mankind.

2.23 *Yin*: the implication seems to be that, just as the Zhou and Yin based themselves on the ritual of the preceding dynasty, so the existence of a constant pattern of ritual ensures that we can forecast the general nature of society a hundred generations hence. It should be remembered that 'ritual' sometimes had a wider than purely religious connotation, and here it means something close to 'cultural traditions'.

3.1 *eight rows of dancers*: to use eight rows of dancers (with eight persons in each row) was a privilege of the Son of Heaven, so the usurpation of this rite by the Ji family, who were not even the legitimate rulers of the state of Lu, was shocking.

3.2 *Yong*: the name of one of the pieces in the *Book of Songs*. As in the previous chapter Master Kong is complaining about the wrongful adoption of rites appropriate to the Son of Heaven by the Three Families who had usurped power in Lu.

3.6 *Ran You*: a disciple of Master Kong who seems to have had administrative ability and to have been particularly interested in government. At this time he was clearly in the service of the Ji family, who were improperly sacrificing to

Mount Tai, one of the sacred mountains. The last sentence implies that Mount Tai is bound to know enough about ritual to reject the sacrifice, so that the suggestion that it is inferior to Lin Fang, who is depicted two chapters earlier as enquiring about the root of ritual, is absurd.

3.8   *plain silk which is made into finery*: the previous two lines occur in *Book of Songs* 57, but this one does not occur. The meaning is that the natural beauty of the girl is afterwards covered in make-up, although the metaphor is changed to that of the ornamentation of materials. The implication assumed by Shang (i.e. Zixia) is that, despite the importance of ritual in putting a gloss on man's actions, it is secondary to the essential human qualities.

3.9   *Qi*: a small state in present-day Henan province (not to be confused with the major state in northern Shandong which is similarly romanized). The descendants of the Xia Dynasty had been enfeoffed there, while Song was the much more important state ruled by the successors of the Yin. The implication seems to be that Master Kong believed that he had much more evidence about Zhou institutions than about the traditions of the other two dynasties.

3.10 *di sacrifice*: an important sacrifice which should only have been performed by the Son of Heaven, but which, to judge from this and the following chapter, was now incorrectly performed and inadequately understood. If properly understood, it held the key to solving the world's problems.

3.12 *sacrifice as if present*: this seems to mean that, although the general view was that during a sacrifice one should show as much reverence as if the spirits themselves were present, the Master thought that the important thing was the attitude of the sacrificer rather than the presence of spirits.

3.13 *south-west corner*: the place of honour in the house, although the stove-god was more closely concerned with the comfort of the family and might be appealed to for more immediate benefit. Wangsun Jia, who was a minister of Wei, quotes this proverb to suggest that it would be better for people to butter him up rather than flatter the ruler. Master Kong will have none of this self-serving philosophy.

3.15 *grand temple*: the temple of the Duke of Zhou, founder of the state of Lu.

3.16   *the leather*: this refers to piercing the leather at the centre
       of the target, which required strength; but, as we have seen,
       archery was regarded as an activity which provided scope
       for ceremonious behaviour rather than for a display of brute
       strength.

3.19   *Duke Ding*: ruler of Lu from 509 to 495 BC.

3.20   *Guan ju*: the first piece in the *Book of Songs*. The moder-
       ation of words and music associated with the *Songs* is much
       approved by Master Kong.

3.21   *Zai Wo*: a disciple of Master Kong who is recorded in
       the *Analects* as being criticized by him on a number of
       occasions.

       tremble: written with the same character as the word for
       'chestnut'. The passage refers to the planting of trees round
       the altar. It appears that Master Kong did not like Zai Wo's
       interpretation of the use of chestnuts, presumably because it
       implied that the revered Zhou had employed terrorism.

3.22   *Guan Zhong*: chief minister of Duke Huan of Qi, who
       reigned from 685 to 643 BC and became first of the para-
       mount princes who headed an alliance of northern Chinese
       states in nominal support of the enfeebled Zhou Dynasty.
       Guan Zhong was regarded as mainly responsible for his
       success, but Master Kong's attitude towards him was
       ambivalent and in the *Mencius* he was attacked as a pro-
       ponent of the use of force rather than virtue in politics.

3.25   *shao*: the music accompanying dances miming the peaceful
       accession of the legendary Shun, whose virtue secured him
       the succession on the abdication of Yao. Its profound
       impact on Master Kong is described at 7.14. The *wu* was
       the music of King Wu who founded the Zhou Dynasty after
       military conquest.

4.1   *neighbourhood*: this chapter is quoted in the *Mencius*.
       Mencius's mother is said to have moved home so that
       her son could live in a neighbourhood permeated with
       humaneness.

4.19   *fixed destination*: so that one can easily be called back in
       case of need.

5.4   *jade sacrificial vessel*: a vessel is designed for a specific
       purpose, rather than having the general qualities appro-
       priate to a gentleman (cf. 2.12), but Master Kong wants
       Zigong to know that he is the most precious type of vessel.

5.5   *Yong*: the disciple Ran Yong who, to judge from other references, was of humble origins but had sufficient ability to occupy the role of a ruler (cf. 6.1 and 6.6).·

5.7   *raft*: Master Kong is only joking when he suggests this means of transport. He has a dig at his disciple's thoughtless desire for action.

5.8   *Qiu*: Ran You, a disciple mentioned frequently later in the book.

      Chi: the disciple Gongxi Hua, who seems elsewhere, as here, to be known particularly for his interest in court ceremonies.

5.13 *way of Heaven*: the natural phenomena as compared with the ways of mankind. The phrase does not occur elsewhere in the *Analects*. Although the reader may be surprised to hear that the Master does not talk about human nature, in fact the word *xing* occurs only this once, although it is much discussed later, e.g. in the *Mencius*.

5.16 *Zichan*: he was chief minister of Zheng and a great statesman of the period.

5.17 *Yan Pingzhong*: after long service to the state he became chief minister of Qi under Duke Jing (ruled 547–490).

5.18 *Zang Wenzhong*: an official in Lu who, despite his good reputation, had evidently incurred the displeasure of Master Kong for living in too grand a style.

5.19 *Ziwen*: a chief minister of Chu during the seventh century BC known for his integrity.

5.20 *Twice will do*: this is the kind of chapter which gives the commentators much scope for ingenious but unconvincing explanation.

5.23 *Bo Yi and Shu Qi*: famous heroes of the end of the Yin Dynasty. Their father had intended the younger to succeed him as lord of a small state, but neither was willing to deprive the other of the succession, so they fled to the mountains and starved themselves to death when the Yin was overthrown by the Zhou, being unwilling to live under a regime established by force.

5.24 *Weisheng Gao*: he was so insistent on keeping his promises that, having said he would meet his girl-friend in the dried-up bed of a stream, he drowned because the water rose before she turned up; but Master Kong had apparently heard something less flattering about him.

5.26 *clothing*: I adopt the reading which omits the word 'light' before 'clothing'.

6.1 *face south*: i.e. given the seat of the ruler. This would have been recorded because it was high praise indeed for one of Master Kong's disciples.

6.4 *Master Ran*: i.e. Ran You, one of only four of Master Kong's disciples who were themselves called Master in the *Analects*.

five bing: Master Ran provides grain for Gongxi Hua's mother. The measures referred to are in ascending order of magnitude. Master Kong clearly objects to her being given a grain allowance, feeling that Gongxi Hua (also referred to in the chapter by his personal name Chi) is quite able to support his own mother. The final allowance represents a firm refusal to accept the Master's view.

6.6 *brindled ox*: this implies that Zhonggong's father was of inferior breed. This should not impede the son's progress, just as the offspring of a brindled ox should not be rejected even if it is pure in colour and thus fit for sacrifice. The spirits of hills and streams would certainly not reject it.

6.9 *Bi*: the stronghold of the Ji family.

Wen: a river on the frontier between Lu and Qi. Being loyal to the legitimate rulers of Lu, he intends to make a getaway rather than serve the usurpers.

6.13 *ru*: this chapter sees the only mention in the *Analects* of the word which later comes to be used for the literati. Given a lack of context and of parallel passages it is not certain what is meant here, although the word is generally taken to have originally referred to people who prized civil rather than military qualities. In English it is often rendered 'Confucian'.

6.15 *Meng Zhifan*: this event is recorded as taking place in 484 BC, when Meng was one of the Lu generals retreating in the face of Qi advances.

6.16 *Zhao*: this handsome prince and the priest Tuo were both contemporaries of Master Kong.

6.22 *keep them at a distance*: ghosts and spirits are kept at a distance by ensuring that their appetites are assuaged with sacrifices, so that they do not interfere in human affairs.

6.25 *gu*: a bronze ritual vessel. The implication is presumably that, although a ritual vessel may be misused, it remains a ritual vessel, whereas a gentleman (a term which presupposes adherence to standards of moral behaviour) does not necessarily always remain a gentleman.

6.28 *Nanzi*: the notorious wife of a ruler of Wei, hence the displeasure of the serious-minded Zilu. The Master's oath implies that he thinks he has done nothing wrong.

6.29 *Mean*: the expression *zhong yong*, here translated as 'Mean', is the title of one of the Confucian books, which is commonly known in English as the *Doctrine of the Mean*. But since this is the only occurrence of this phrase in the *Analects* and it comes in a very brief extract, its meaning here cannot be certain.

6.30 *Yao and Shun*: famous legendary sage-kings.

7.1 *Peng*: it is unfortunately not clear who he was. The first sentence is one of the most famous in the *Analects*. In hostile eyes it is a slogan of rigid conservatism, but not only Master Kong but many others have proved that much good can arise from presenting ancient ways imaginatively to a contemporary audience.

7.5 *Duke of Zhou*: brother of King Wu, founder of the Zhou Dynasty, and regent during the reign of his nephew King Cheng. He was founder of the ruling house of Lu and hence a great hero of the early Zhou period. Master Kong saw him as a model. Although in this passage his failure to dream of the Duke of Zhou reflects his disillusionment, dreaming of the dead often implied that the ghost was hungry and wanted sacrificing to.

7.7 *bundle of dried meat*: the humblest of presents. Master Kong was prepared to teach anyone, however poor. The following chapter however indicates that he expected enthusiastic participation from his pupils.

7.11 *in store*: the Chinese word means 'to hide', but in the only other passage in which it occurs (9.13) it refers to storing the precious jewel of one's talent, so I have used the same translation here.

three armies: a major state had three armies.

7.12 *fellow carrying a whip*: i.e. a humble attendant.

7.15   *Lord of Wei*: he was trying to hold on to the sovereignty of
        the state which should rightfully have been his father's.
        Master Kong could not admire anyone who had behaved so
        differently from such model renouncers as Bo Yi and Shu
        Qi, but direct criticism is avoided by the method still
        familiar in China.

7.18   *standard pronunciation*: instead of using Lu dialect.

7.21   *did not speak of*: naturally this is taken by commentators
        and translators as a generalization, but it could perhaps
        more plausibly refer to a single incident.

7.23   *Huan Tui*: the Song Minister of War, who had attempted
        to kill him. This sounds like the sort of remark which would
        have been attributed to Master Kong after the legend had
        developed.

7.27   *corded arrow*: with a string attached so that it could be
        retrieved.

7.28   *inferior variety of knowledge*: this chapter seems sarcastic,
        but there are other references to the superiority of innate
        knowledge (e.g. 16.9).

7.29   *purifies himself*: it was necessary for a suppliant to purify
        himself with fasting and abstinence.

7.31   *Wu Meng Zi*: this means the eldest one of the Zi surname
        from Wu. The ducal houses of Wu and Lu both had the Ji
        surname, so Duke Zhao, who reigned over Lu from 541 to
        509 BC, was breaking the rule of exogamy. To try to hide
        his solecism he called his wife Zi, which was the surname of
        the ducal house of Song. Master Kong is being blamed for
        saying that Duke Zhao understood the rites when he was in
        clear breach of them. Perhaps he did not want to be heard
        criticizing his late sovereign.

7.35   *for a long time*: i.e. it is sufficient for him to be judged by
        the life he has led, so it is not necessary to pray for him.

8.1   *Tai Bo*: great-uncle of King Wu, who founded the Zhou
        Dynasty. He fled because, although he was the eldest son
        and should have ruled over the Zhou people, he realized
        that his father had other intentions. He became founder of
        the state of Wu in the south. Since the Zhou Dynasty had
        not yet been founded, it is wrong to say that he 'renounced
        the right to rule over all under Heaven'.

8.3 *came through safely*: Master Zeng, who was renowned for his filial piety, was glad that he had gone through life preserving his body intact, this being one of the principle duties of a filial son. The *Song* is quoted as words fit to describe a filial son's state of anxiety to make sure that he performs his duties correctly.

8.5 *my friend*: the traditional view was that this referred to Yan Hui.

8.12 *intent on*: a suitable slogan for today's undergraduates starting non-vocational courses! This interpretation does involve the acceptance of an alternative reading to give 'intent on' instead of 'reach', but this makes much better sense.

8.18 *Yu*: like Shun, he was an ancient sage-king. He was renowned for saving China from floods (as referred to in 8.21). He received the throne from Shun because of his virtues and was reckoned to have been the founder of the Xia Dynasty.

8.20 *virtue of Zhou*: called perfect because, under Wu, the Zhou people remained subservient although they already controlled a large area of all under Heaven. There does not seem to be any necessary connection between this point and that about the rarity of political skills made in the first part of the chapter.

8.21 *devotion*: in supplying plentiful sacrificial food in contrast with his own personal abstemiousness.

9.1 *1*: this chapter has made commentators adopt all kinds of tortuous explanations, especially since it seems from the *Analects* that he referred to 'humaneness' frequently. But one must remember that the fact that this is paradoxical does not militate against its being recorded.

9.2 *take up charioteering*: a sarcastic response to the failure to appreciate that the gentleman is a generalist rather than a specialist.

9.3 *ascending*: mounting the dais on which the ruler would be seated in the audience-hall.

9.5 *Kuang*: a town where Master Kong was supposed to have been mistaken for an adventurer called Yang Huo. The implication of this passage is that Master Kong was the sole repository of culture. King Wen means literally 'the cultured

King', but culture evidently survived his death, although it would not survive Master Kong's. This passage evidently comes from a source which already sees Master Kong as a culture hero.

9.9   *chart*: the phoenix and the chart were omens whose appearance was said to foretell the coming of a sage. The 'chart' refers to the occasion when a monster rose from the river carrying on its back markings which inspired Fu Xi, the most ancient of the sage-emperors, to invent writing.

9.10 *made haste*: a sign of respect.

9.11 *it*: Master Kong's teaching. This is a classic account of the disciples' admiration.

9.12 *official underlings*: not holding office, he was not entitled to such.

9.13 *beautiful jade*: the question is whether the possessor of political talent (for which 'beautiful jade' is a metaphor) should be prepared to take office even in these inauspicious times. To judge from the *Analects* Master Kong generally maintains the impractical stance that one should not take part in government 'if the Way does not prevail'. Sometimes, however, he is depicted as being more realistic, but here perhaps he is being a little facetious, as indeed in the next chapter.

9.15 *the ya and the song*: sections of the *Book of Songs*, which later tradition credited Master Kong with editing.

9.21 *stopping*: because he was overtaken by premature death he never in fact stopped in his progress.

9.27 *these lines*: from *Song* 33. We do not of course know how the Master interpreted the poem, but it is a short piece in which a wife bewails the absence of her husband. It seems that the lady is reproaching him by saying: 'I am neither wicked nor greedy, so why are you not good?'

9.31 *31*: lacking a context, this chapter's interpretation is obscure and the quotation sounds like the *Book of Songs* but does not exist in the present version.

10   *Book 10*: this book is different in character from the others and is an account of ritual behaviour partly ascribed to the gentleman and partly to Master Kong. It may derive from followers who gave greater stress to the performance of correct ritual than Master Kong did and it has therefore

been regarded by some as an interpolation, but there is nothing in it which seems to be totally at odds with the rest of the book, which is in any case a motley collection. Indeed there are chapters elsewhere in the *Analects* which are very reminiscent of this book, e.g. 7.4, 9, 10, and 27.

10.8   *eastern steps*: the position of a host receiving guests.

10.13   *head to the east*: the proper position of a sick person.

10.20   *20*: this and the following chapter consist of unintelligible fragments.

11.3   *virtuous conduct*: evidently this chapter consists of notes made by someone other than Master Kong concerning the talents of some of the disciples.

11.6   *white jade sceptre*: the lines from *Book of Songs* 256 which say that, although a flaw in a white jade sceptre can be polished away, a flaw in words cannot be removed. A different reason is given for this betrothal at 5.2.

11.8   *Yan Lu*: Yan Hui's father. Presumably, relying on the Master's great affection for Yan Hui, he asked him to trade his carriage for an outer coffin, but Master Kong's rejoinder is that his own son Li did not have an outer coffin when he died, and that it would be improper for himself on such an occasion to be without a carriage.

11.12   *serving men*: this simple statement of Master Kong's humanism is often quoted.

11.13   *You*: the reference to Zilu is plausible in view of his temperament (and in fact he did meet a violent death), but does not fit with the context, so a hiatus seems likely.

11.15   *You's zither*: the disciples apparently assumed that their Master was implying that Zilu did not deserve to be a member of his school, but Master Kong indicates that Zilu has made some progress.

11.17   *sound the drum*: in ancient China the drum was sounded to order troops to advance. The usage here is of course metaphorical.

11.18   *Chai*: there is only one other reference to him in the *Analects* (11.23), but the other three are better known—Master Zeng, Zizhang, and Zilu. The words 'the Master said' are evidently missing. This saying was presumably treasured because of the extremely unflattering epithets used. The second half of the chapter, as indeed is the case with 19, appears to have no connection with the first.

11.23　*Zigao*: he was made steward of Bi by Zilu, who was steward of the Ji family. Master Kong disapproves because Bi is the stronghold of the Ji usurpers, although it is noticeable that Zilu has utilized a favourite argument of Master Kong.

11.24　*Zeng Xi*: the father of Master Zeng, he is not elsewhere mentioned in the *Analects*. His personal name is Dian and it is his carefree ambition which is most approved by the Master, who must have been caught at a time when he was feeling rather bored with politics.

　　　dancing sacrifice: this was a rain-seeking sacrifice.

12.5　*Sima Niu*: the one known to history had several brothers, so either he is disowning them or this passage refers to a different Sima Niu. 'All within the four seas are brothers' is a well-known Confucian tag, but it is not in fact a saying attributed to Master Kong himself.

12.7　*trust*: this is one of the most famous Confucian sayings, vividly stressing the importance of trust.

12.10　*Not . . . a change*: this quotation from *Book of Songs* 188 about a wife complaining of her husband's interest in a new woman does not seem to fit here.

12.11　*let a ruler be a ruler*: at a time of usurpations and attempted usurpations such an exchange of views is natural, but it has become one of the key passages in the so-called 'rectification of names' controversy. Since this doctrine is one of the main concerns of the Legalist philosophers a couple of centuries later, some commentators have unnecessarily regarded this passage as anachronistic. In fact the correct application of names, e.g. humaneness, is one of the principal topics of the *Analects*. On the rectification of names see also 13.3.

12.12　*avoided sleeping on a promise*: it was in Zilu's headstrong nature not to put things off, even if this meant making decisions on partial evidence or fulfilling promises before nightfall.

12.17　*to govern means to correct*: the words for 'govern' and 'correct' are both pronounced the same and are related.

12.19　*small man*: notice that it is not the *people*, but the *small man* who bends.

12.22 *Gao Yao*: he was a wise minister of Shun, and Yi Yin was a wise minister of Tang, the founder of the Yin Dynasty.

13.3 *rectify names*: the word here translated 'rectify' is again the word *zheng* (correct) which, as we have seen, is related to *zheng* (government). Rites and music are linked with punishment because the latter is the constraint which has to be used to control the people, who cannot be guided by the example enshrined in ritual behaviour and celebrated in music. Although the sentiments are not alien to the *Analects*, the style of the passage, with its elaborate chain-argument, appears late. (In his second speech Master Kong addresses Zilu by his personal name You, but I have excluded it because of the confusion which would be caused by the presence in the same sentence of the English second person pronoun.)

13.4 *will come to him*: the task of the ruler was conceived as ruling justly and benevolently so that migrants were attracted from other states to boost the population.

13.7 *brothers*: at the beginning of the Zhou Dynasty two sons of King Wen were enfeoffed with Lu and Wei, so Master Kong is making the point that their regimes show a fraternal similarity.

13.12 *true king*: apart from a couple of places where the 'former kings' are mentioned, the word for king (*wang*) does not occur anywhere else in the *Analects*. Its use is similar to that in the *Mencius*, where *wang* means the one who rules by virtue rather than force. I have therefore rendered it by 'true king'. Although this usage is unique in the *Analects*, this passage does enhance the doctrine of the transforming power of the virtuous ruler by supplying it with the authority of Master Kong.

13.14 *government business*: this incident may have occurred when Master Ran was working for the usurping Ji family, which had no authority to preside over government business.

13.18 *fathers cover up for their sons*: this encapsulates the Chinese regard for the importance of the family as compared with the state. Informing against parents in antiquity, as more recently in the Cultural Revolution, represents the antithesis of Confucian values.

13.22 *constancy*: this is a quotation from the *Book of Changes* concerning the hexagram for 'constancy'. Presumably the import of the Master's final remark is that, although the *Book of Changes* has something pertinent on constancy, people are aware of its importance without divination.

13.29 *seven years*: this may seem a long time but the view is that people should have a thorough instruction in morality before being asked to take up arms. This is the sense behind the following chapter also.

14.1 *1*: the second paragraph does not have any obvious connection with the first, so in some translations it appears as a separate chapter.

14.5 *Ji*: he did not in fact gain possession of all under Heaven, but was the ancestor of the Zhou people who achieved this many centuries later. Yi was the most famous archer of antiquity and Ao was renowned for his physical strength.

14.8 *dispatches were prepared*: in the state of Zheng.

14.9 *Bo*: the implication is that Guan Zhong could get away with anything. At the beginning of this speech I have omitted 'he was a man'. It looks as if an adjective descriptive of Guan Zhong has dropped out of the text.

14.11 *Meng Gongchuo*: he was in fact a grandee in Lu, but Master Kong says that he would be all right as comptroller of an important family, but would be no use as an official even in a minor state.

14.12 *complete man*: this expression does not occur elsewhere in the *Analects*.

14.14 *Zang Wuzhong*: a Lu grandee who tried to persuade the Duke of Lu to allow his brother Wei to succeed him as holder of the fief of Fang.

14.15 *Duke Wen*: he reigned over Jin from 636 to 628 BC, and was the second of the princes who headed the league of northern states. Duke Huan of Qi had been the first.

14.16 *Prince Jiu*: Duke Huan's brother. Shao Hu, like Guan Zhong, was an adviser of Duke Huan.

14.17 *wearing our hair down and fastening our clothes on the left*: barbarian practices.

14.18 *cultured*: the posthumous title *wen*, which comes in Wenzi, means 'cultured'. Gongshu Wenzi had evidently secured the promotion of Zhuan at the same time as himself.

14.21 *Duke Jian*: this ruler of Qi was murdered in 481 BC. Punishment would have involved the use of military force. The 'Three' are the heads of the three families who held power in Lu.

14.24 *for the sake of others*: i.e. to impress others.

14.32 *Qiu*: Weisheng Mu impolitely addresses Master Kong by his personal name.

14.37 *seven men*: this sentence makes no sense and seems out of place here.

14.39 *beats the chimes with feeling*: this is taken to mean that the Master's frustration shows in his playing. The quotation below, from *Book of Songs* 34, implies that one should take things as one finds them. Master Kong's response is at first sarcastic, but then he affirms his commitment.

14.40 *Gao Zong*: a ruler of the Yin Dynasty.

15.3 *one thing*: it is held by some that an explanation is to be found in 4.15.

15.5 *non-action*: the expression used here is *wu wei*, which is generally associated with Daoism.

15.11 *sounds of Zheng*: the popular music of the state of Zheng.

15.14 *Liu Xia Hui*: a seventh-century Lu official who was greatly esteemed by Confucians.

15.20 *reputation*: this may seem to be in conflict with the preceding chapter, but however unconcerned one may be about recognition during one's lifetime, it is a matter of filial piety to bring glory on one's parents by leaving a good reputation after one's death.

15.22 *parties*: this chapter provided a good text for hostility to factionalism in imperial China.

15.25 *three dynasties*: the Xia, Yin, and Zhou, which are said to have followed the straightforward Way for the sake of the people. Similarly any praiseworthy person must have taken the interests of the people as a criterion.

15.26 *26*: I have translated this chapter as closely as possible but the meaning is a matter of speculation. The two sentences may not belong together.

15.39 *categorization*: this brief saying is obscure, but it has generally been taken to mean that there are no class-distinctions in education. The word *lei* (categorization) does not occur elsewhere in the *Analects*.

15.42 *music-master*: these were generally blind.

16.1 *Zhuanyu*: a small dependency of the state of Lu. Master Kong objects to Ran You and Zilu, who are in the employ of the Ji family, conniving at an attack on a place which had been entrusted with an important state sacrifice by the Zhou founders.

upheavals: this sentence is difficult and probably corrupt.

16.2 *lost*: the subject of 'lost' must be the system of rites, music, and punitive expeditions. The passage is characterized by artificiality, which suggests that it is comparatively late. The numbered sets (in this case 'generations') occurring in this and many other chapters in this book and also in Books 17 and 20 do not feature at all in the earlier books, which are apparently more authentic.

16.3 *three Huan*: the three families who controlled Lu are thus called because they were descended from a Duke of Lu called Huan.

16.12 *no opportunity to offer him praise*: this phrase is used at 8.1, there referring to Tai Bo. Here the meaning is different: they had no opportunity because there was nothing to praise, whereas in the case of Tai Bo the people had no opportunity because he had disappeared.

the saying: the chapter is incomplete, for there is no saying to which this refers. Normally too one would have expected some such expression as 'the Master said' at the beginning of the chapter.

16.13 *Boyu*: Master Kong's son.

hurriedly: as we have seen before, quick movement was a sign of deference.

16.14 *14*: this chapter is clearly from a text on etiquette and does not belong to the *Analects*.

17.1 *one's treasure*: as elsewhere talent is regarded as something very precious, but at the end of this chapter Master Kong is depicted as willing to serve even a usurper.

17.2 *to each other*: although there are no discussions of human nature in the *Analects*, this brief saying is taken as evidence that the Master believed that the influence of nurture was greater than of nature.

17.3　*ox-knife*: this remark of Master Kong is intended to suggest that it was a waste of effort to teach music to the locals, but he accepts Ziyou's objection.

17.4　*Zhou in the East*: i.e. a Zhou in Master Kong's own state of Lu. The original Zhou Dynasty had its capital near the present Xi'an in the west of China. The historical reference is obscure, but it looks as if Master Kong feels that this rebellion against the Ji usurpers may restore the legitimate rulers of Lu and give him the prospect of being able to establish a regime like the golden age of the early Zhou Dynasty.

17.6　*bitter gourd*: a potent symbol of Master Kong's frustration at not obtaining employment. This time, as cf. 17.1 and 17.4, the employment would have been in the state of Jin rather than in his native state of Lu. The sayings about grinding and dyeing are meant to indicate the Master's incorruptibility.

17.8　*Zhounan and Shaonan*: first two books of the *Book of Songs*.

17.9　*ritual*: a classic summary of the view that the significance of ritual and music does not lie simply in their outward manifestations.

17.11　*village worthy*: the reasons for the saying are given in *Mencius* 7b37. The essence is that, since they are praised by the multitude, village worthies always believe themselves to be right and cannot be brought to approach the Way.

17.12　*rejection of virtue*: presumably because one should proclaim truths on the highways.

17.16　*vermilion*: the correct ritual colour. The sharp tongues expressing dangerous views serve as a parallel. The modern equivalent would be a dislike of pop music drowning classical music, and the predomination of presentational skills rather than ideological convictions in politics.

　　　sounds of Zheng: Master Kong's antipathy to music from the state of Zheng is also mentioned in 15.11.

17.17　*What ever does Heaven say?*: the striking thing about this chapter is that Master Kong is depicted as comparing himself with Heaven.

17.19   *three years' mourning*: although the Master's justification of three years' mourning is absurd, this passage helped to ensure that his support for the practice became enshrined in the Confucian tradition.

   drills have made new fire: this refers to a ritual procedure for rekindling fire in the spring.

17.20   *bo and yi*: both board-games, the latter being the equivalent of *weiqi* (or *go* in Japanese).

17.23   *women*: commentators of course attempt to soften the misogyny.

18.1   *him*: Zhou, the last bad ruler of the Yin Dynasty. The people mentioned were all relatives of his and were regarded by the Master as humane.

18.3   *the Ji and the Meng*: two of the three powerful noble houses in Lu.

18.4   *Ji Huan Zi*: the member of the Ji family who held power in Lu from 505 to 492 BC.

18.6   *knows the way across*: a sarcastic response. Since he is a sage, he must know everything.

   change places with him: as things stand I am tempted to become a recluse like Jieni, but I would not if the Way prevailed.

18.8   *8*: this chapter seems corrupt and the remaining three chapters of this book seem to be stray fragments which do not belong to the text.

   19   *Book 19*: the reader will notice that, although Master Kong is mentioned and even quoted in this book, it consists of sayings and dialogues of disciples and others.

19.12   *embraces both beginning and end*: Ziyou's argument is that one must start off with elementary matters rather than fundamental principles, since only the sage is capable of encompassing the whole at once.

19.20   *Zhou's*: he was the wicked last ruler of the Yin Dynasty who was overthrown by King Wu the founder of the Zhou Dynasty. (The second Zhou is written with a different character from the first.)

19.22   *Zhongni*: i.e. Master Kong.

19.23   *ren*: about 8 feet.

19.25   *saying*: no source is given for this eulogy. The ecstatic references to the Master in these last three chapters plainly date from a time when the legend took precedence over reality.

20.1   *1*: this chapter seems to consist of disconnected fragments from a work resembling the *Book of Documents*.

INDEX

Roman numerals refer to page numbers in the Introduction; arabic numerals refer to books and chapters in the text or, in the case of numbers 83–103, to the Notes. Where a second chapter in a book appears, only the chapter number is given.

THE WORLD'S CLASSICS

A Select List

HANS ANDERSEN: Fairy Tales
Translated by L. W. Kingsland
Introduction by Naomi Lewis
Illustrated by Vilhelm Pedersen and Lorenz Frølich

ARTHUR J. ARBERRY (Transl.): The Koran

LUDOVICO ARIOSTO: Orlando Furioso
Translated by Guido Waldman

ARISTOTLE: The Nicomachean Ethics
Translated by David Ross

JANE AUSTEN: Emma
Edited by James Kinsley and David Lodge

Mansfield Park
Edited by James Kinsley and John Lucas

Northanger Abbey, Lady Susan, The Watsons,
and Sanditon
Edited by John Davie

HONORÉ DE BALZAC: Père Goriot
Translated and Edited by A. J. Krailsheimer

CHARLES BAUDELAIRE: The Flowers of Evil
Translated by James McGowan
Introduction by Jonathan Culler

WILLIAM BECKFORD: Vathek
Edited by Roger Lonsdale

R. D. BLACKMORE: Lorna Doone
Edited by Sally Shuttleworth

KEITH BOSLEY (Transl.): The Kalevala

ORIENTAL TALES
Edited by Robert L. Mack

OVID: Metamorphoses
Translated by A. D. Melville
Introduction and Notes by E. J. Kenney

FRANCESCO PETRARCH:
Selections from the Canzoniere and Other Works
Translated by Mark Musa

EDGAR ALLAN POE: Selected Tales
Edited by Julian Symons

JEAN RACINE: Britannicus, Phaedra, Athaliah
Translated by C. H. Sisson

ANN RADCLIFFE: The Italian
Edited by Frederick Garber

The Mysteries of Udolpho
Edited by Bonamy Dobrée

The Romance of the Forest
Edited by Chloe Chard

THE MARQUIS DE SADE:
The Misfortune of Virtue and Other Early Tales
Translated and Edited by David Coward

PAUL SALZMAN (Ed.):
An Anthology of Elizabethan Prose Fiction

OLIVE SCHREINER: The Story of an African Farm
Edited by Joseph Bristow

SIR WALTER SCOTT: The Heart of Midlothian
Edited by Claire Lamont

Waverley
Edited by Claire Lamont

HORACE WALPOLE : The Castle of Otranto
Edited by W. S. Lewis

IZAAK WALTON and CHARLES COTTON:
The Compleat Angler
Edited by John Buxton
Introduction by John Buchan

OSCAR WILDE: Complete Shorter Fiction
Edited by Isobel Murray

The Picture of Dorian Gray
Edited by Isobel Murray

MARY WOLLSTONECRAFT:
Mary *and* The Wrongs of Woman
Edited by Gary Kelly

VIRGINIA WOOLF: Mrs Dalloway
Edited by Claire Tomalin

Orlando
Edited by Rachel Bowlby

ÉMILE ZOLA:
The Attack on the Mill and Other Stories
Translated by Douglas Parmée

Nana
Translated and Edited by Douglas Parmée

A complete list of Oxford Paperbacks, including The World's Classics, OPUS, Past Masters, Oxford Authors, Oxford Shakespeare, and Oxford Paperback Reference, is available in the UK from the Arts and Reference Publicity Department (BH), Oxford University Press, Walton Street, Oxford OX2 6DP.

In the USA, complete lists are available from the Paperbacks Marketing Manager, Oxford University Press, 200 Madison Avenue, New York, NY 10016.

Oxford Paperbacks are available from all good bookshops. In case of difficulty, customers in the UK can order direct from Oxford University Press Bookshop, Freepost, 116 High Street, Oxford, OX1 4BR, enclosing full payment. Please add 10 per cent of published price for postage and packing.